IMAGES
*of Sport*

# WALSALL
## FOOTBALL CLUB

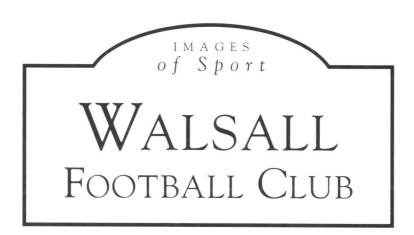

IMAGES
*of Sport*

# WALSALL
## FOOTBALL CLUB

*Compiled by*
Geoff Allman

TEMPUS

Tempus Publishing Limited
The Mill, Brimscombe Port,
Stroud, Gloucestershire, GL5 2QG

ISBN 0 7524 2091 7

Typesetting and origination by
Tempus Publishing Limited
Printed in Great Britain by
Midway Clark Printing, Wiltshire

## Also available from Tempus Publishing

| | | |
|---|---|---|
| *Birmingham City FC* | Tony Matthews | 0 7524 1862 9 |
| *Crewe Alexandra FC* | Harold Finch | 0 7524 1545 X |
| *Crystal Palace FC* | Nigel Sands | 0 7524 1544 1 |
| *Forever England* | Mark Shaoul/Tony Williamson | 0 7524 2042 9 |
| *Leeds United FC* | David Saffer | 0 7524 1642 1 |
| *Manchester City FC* | David Saffer | 0 7524 2085 2 |
| | | |
| *Leicestershire CCC* | Dennis Lambert | 0 7524 1864 5 |
| *Worcestershire CCC* | Les Hatton | 0 7524 1834 3 |
| | | |
| *Final Tie* | Norman Shiel | 0 7524 1669 3 |
| *The Five Nations Story* | David Hands | 0 7524 1851 3 |
| *The Football Programme* | John Litster | 0 7524 1855 6 |
| *Speedway in East Anglia* | Norman Jacobs | 0 7524 1882 3 |
| *St Andrews Golfing Legends* | Stuart Marshall | 0 7524 1812 2 |
| *Voices of 1966* | Norman Shiel | 0 7524 2045 3 |

This is just a small selection of our sports titles. For a full catalogue please contact
the Sales Department at the address given above. Alternatively you can telephone
on 01453 883300 or e-mail sales@tempus-publishing.com.

# Contents

The greatest name in the history of Walsall Football Club is that of Gilbert Alsop, the centre forward who was signed from Coventry in September 1931. He scored on his debut against Doncaster Rovers and fourteen months later headed the opening goal in Walsall's greatest ever win – against Arsenal in the FA Cup. Though he moved to West Bromwich in November 1935, he returned to Walsall via Ipswich in time to score 17 goals in the last seven games of 1938/39. He retired as a player at the age of forty and later served the club for many years as groundsman.

# Introduction

19 February 1944 was a significant day in my life as I was taken, at the age of eight, by my dad to a wartime game between Walsall and Wolves at the old Fellows Park ground. I can still see in my mind's eye Walsall goalkeeper Bert Williams saving a header from Dickie Dorset right on half-time and Bernard Streten, who was guesting for Wolves, saving a penalty from George Dudley.

Soon I was old enough to go unescorted and I thrilled to the Walsall team of the early post-war years with Dave Massart banging home hat-tricks galore, diminutive Jackie Lewis keeping goal with skill, agility and courage and Doug Lishman and Dennis Wilshaw, destined to reach the heights with Arsenal and Wolves respectively, forming the left flank of the attack.

I recall the many friendly fans I was privileged to stand next to at the Hillary Street end and the times I ran all the way from school two miles away to see the second half of Thursday afternoon games. There have been so many high moments, such as successive promotion years in the early 1960s, the FA Cup goals scored by Bernie Wright, Alan Buckley and George Andrews as Manchester United and Newcastle were beaten in 1975 and the way Mark Rees's blistering pace frightened Liverpool at Anfield in 1984. There have also been the sad times – the relegation in May 1963 after a serious injury to goalkeeper Alan Boswell in the final game against Charlton and the brave but unavailing battle against relegation in May 2000.

But the spirit of Walsall Football Club is unquenchable and it has never been greater than under current boss Ray Graydon as we all prepare to roar the Saddlers on to future glories that may ultimately exceed the many great days that are recalled in this publication.

Geoff Allman
September 2000

# Acknowledgements

I would like to place on record the kindness of the *Express and Star* and *Birmingham Post and Mail* and local photographer and former Football League linesman Don Stanton for allowing the extensive use of photographs from their respective libraries. I am particularly grateful to Fran Cartwright, Paul Marston, Peter Willis, Ron Jukes and Mike Bondy for their unfailing support. I also owe debts that can never be repaid to sports writers past and present (particularly to dear old Bill Rowlinson who wrote about Walsall FC for over half a century) whose writings have underpinned my love of Walsall FC. Finally, thanks to the hundreds of players whose skill and enthusiasm have made Walsall FC the great club that it is and to the thousands of fans who have shared my enthusiasm over the years.

Bescot Stadium, which opened in 1990, is the fourth ground on which Walsall have played regular League football. The first-ever League game was played on the Chuckery Ground in 1892, the West Bromwich Road ground was used from 1893 to 1896 and the Hillary Street ground (renamed Fellows Park) from 1896 to 1990. As an emergency measure, Walsall also used the Wood Green Oval in 1893, briefly returned to West Bromwich Road in 1900/01 and used the Hawthorns for one game in 1970.

# One
# The Early Years

WALSALL VICTORIA v. WEDNESBURY OLD PARK.—
A match between the above clubs was played on
Saturday last, at Walsall. The following were the
players:—*Victoria*: Messrs W. Robinson (captain),
J. Robinson, T. Spriggs, J. Spriggs, Tapper, Stokes,
Hawley, D. Bray, G. Bray, Dallard, Draper, Taylor,
Wallace, Careless and Mason. *Old Park*: Messrs
Benton (captain), Holland, Jay, Dean, Minific,
Stokes, Morley, Hill, Cooper, Lowe, Wilkins, Speed,
Daniels, Reeves and Horton. Play commenced at
3-30, when Dean started the ball for the visitors.
The game went on till half-time, and, no goal having
been obtained, the sides changed ends—T. Spriggs
kicking off the ball for the Victoria. The Victoria
team made two or three attempts to secure a goal but
failed to do so. Stokes, on behalf of the Victoria,
took the ball from the middle of the field, passing
several men on his way, up to the visitor's goal, but
the goal keeper (Lowe) succeeded in stopping him
from kicking a goal. On time being called, no goal
had been secured, and the match ended in a draw, in
favour of the Victoria. The playing of the following
was worthy of mention:—Messrs. W. Robinson,
Stokes, Tapper and Dallard on behalf of the
Victoria; and Messrs. Dean, Morley and Reeves for
the Old Park.

WALSALL v. BURTON (ROBIN HOODS) — These
clubs played at Burton, on Saturday last, and a well-
contested game of an hour and a half resulted in a
draw; each side having obtained a goal. The
ground was very slippery and the Burton men being
much less than their opponents, were enabled to play
better upon it. Burton obtained a goal twenty
minutes from the time the ball was kicked off, and
although they made one or two attempts to get
another, play was pretty even until the call of half-
time. Ends were then changed, and after about
twenty minutes hard play J. Russell made a capital
rush up the field, and Adams, making the best use of
the chase, secured a goal for the Walsall men, amid
loud cheers from the spectators. The Burton men
redoubled their efforts to obtain another goal but
without success, and the Walsall men left Burton
well pleased that their previous conquerors were not
able again to defeat them.

The present Walsall FC came into existence in 1888 as a result of an amalgamation between
Walsall Swifts (originally known as Victoria Swifts), founded in 1873, and Walsall Town,
founded in 1874. Games were keenly contested though goals were often scarce and for a time
the Swifts played on a ground in Follyhouse Lane and the Town played at The Chuckery, home
matches usually being on alternate weeks.

## FOOTBALL.

### DUMBARTON (SCOTLAND) v. WALSALL SWIFTS.

This important match took place on Saturday last, on the Chuckery Ground, Walsall. What promised to be a beautiful day in the early part of the morning turned out one of the most wretched days imaginable for out-door athletics and pastimes; yet, despite the fact of a pouring rain, so great was the interest manifested in this or.ounter that, by the time play commenced, there must have been between 1,000 and 2,000 persons present. The Swifts won the toss, and chose to kick uphill, with the wind in their favour; and at 3·10 Lindsay started the ball for the visitors. For the first few minutes the play was pretty even, and for some time neither team appeared to hold any particular advantage. The first incident of note was a foul in front of the Swifts' goal for the Dumbarton, but Ashwell cleared the leather away, and for some time the play was confined to the visitors' quarters. Miller at length broke away with the ball and endeavoured to centre to Lindsay, but Yates met it and headed it back. Brandrick was next conspicuous by a run on the right-wing, but Hutcheson tackled him, and the result was a throw-in for the Swifts. Brandrick took the throw, and placed the leather magnificently between the posts; but, as it had not been touched by another player, no score resulted. The home forwards again attacked the visitors' goal, and Brandrick obtained a corner, placing the ball right in the mouth of goal, and a sharp scrimmage took place, but the Scotch backs managed to clear the danger away. A neat bit of passing by the Dumbarton forwards, in which Miller, Lindsay, and Kennedy were prominent, transferred the ball into the home quarters, and Hobson had to use his hands to stop a shot from Lindsay. Lunn obtained possession of the leather, took it up the field, and passed to Farmer, who kicked outside. Brandrick next came in for attention by a clever run on the right, but Lang stopped his progress, and returned the ball to Miller, who, with the assistance of Kennedy, got the leather in front of the home territory. Meikleham shot at goal, and the ball just scraped the outside of the post. Another shot was immediately afterwards made, but Hobson was on the alert, and punched it out in fine style. Sheldon at length got the ball out of danger, and passed to Dyoss, who quickly took it up the field and endeavoured to place it in front of goal, but the wind carried it into touch. Brown then made a pretty run down the centre, but Jones met him and returned the leather. The Swifts had a throw-in, and Lunn, obtaining possession of the ball, dashed off with it, and, averting the Dumbarton backs, by a splendid shot obtained the first goal for the Swifts amidst great cheering. From the kick-off the Scotchmen became the attacking party, and obtained a corner, which was well taken by Brown, but the excellent defence of the home backs frustrated their efforts to score. On changing ends the Dumbarton, with the wind in their favour, were soon busy round the Swifts' goal, and obtained three corner-kicks in rapid succession, but nothing came of them. M'Aulay made a splendid long shot, but the irrepressible Hobson was equal to the occasion, and again threw it out. Kerr returned the ball to Brown, who ran it up close to goal, but, before he had time to make his final shot, Jones was at him and cleared the leather away. Farmer obtained the ball and started off with it at a good pace, but Lang stopped his progress, and by a splendid long kick placed the ball well up the field. Miller got possession of the leather, and gave it to Brown, who put it between the posts, but the goal was objected to on the ground that Miller was off-side when he played the ball, and on an appeal to the referee he decided as "no goal." This gave rise to an angry altercation, and the Dumbarton threatened to leave the field, but after a delay of about five minutes they very wisely consented to continue the game. On resuming operations, the Scotchmen again attacked the home goal, and several times came very near scoring, but the excellent defence of Hobson, Jones, and Sheldon completely baffled the visitors' forwards. Corner after corner fell to the Dumbarton, and shot after shot was made, but Hobson repulsed the attacks, and was greatly cheered for the grand style in which he saved his charge on many occasions. At this point of the game Lunn, who had received a severe kick on the leg, had to retire. For the last fifteen minutes it was so dark that it was almost impossible to discern the ball ten yards away,

but the visitors played with great pluck and determination. The excitement towards the end of the game became tremendous, and speculation was rife as to whether the visitors would score or not. However, three minutes before the call of time the Scotchmen were rewarded for their untiring efforts. Meikleham, coming up with a rush, put in a low shot, which Hobson failed to stop, thus making matters equal. Time was immediately afterwards called, and the match resulted in a tie—one goal each—after an exciting and evenly-contested game. The teams were as follows:—Swifts: Goal, Hobson; back, Jones; three-quarter back, Sheldon; half-back, E. Dyoss (captain), Yates, and Ashwell; forwards, Brandrick, H. Dyoss, Farmer, Tapper, and Lunn. Dumbarton: Goal, J. Kennedy; backs, Lang and Hutcheson; half-backs, P. Miller (captain) and Kerr; forwards, Meikleham, Brown, Lindsay, M'Aulay, J. Miller, and A. Kennedy. Umpires, Messrs. Campbell (Dumbarton) and Dallard (Swifts); referee, Mr. Durban (Aston Unity).

WALSALL v. STAFFORD ROAD.—Played at Wolverhampton on Saturday last. The visitors' team was rather weak, owing to the absence of four of their regular first team players, who were playing at Stoke for their county against North Wales. Their places were well supplied, however, and after a well-contested match Walsall were hailed the winners by four goals to three. Unfortunately the Walsall back player missed his train, and for about twenty minutes Stafford Road held a slight advantage, having only ten men opposed to them, and scored the first goal. Walsall shortly afterwards dashed away, and made matters equal. Again Stafford Road scored, and Walsall followed their example a second time. Reynolds now arrived, and Stone, who had been playing well at half-back, took his own proper position forward. Stafford Road, still keeping the lead, obtained another goal, and the game became more exciting than ever. Walsall played with great determination, and at length obtained their third goal, making matters again equal. Immediately upon the kick-off, the Walsall players secured the ball and ran it right up to the Stafford Road goal. Ray ran out to Dodsworth, but this player unselfishly and cleverly gave the ball to Hill, and by him the winning point was obtained. Upon re-starting, Walsall still pressed their opponents, and a shot from Dodsworth missed by about a foot. No more goals were obtained up to the call of time, and therefore victory rested with the Walsall team by four goals to three. The following were the players:—Walsall: Roberts, goal; Reynolds, Tucker, backs; Tonks, H. Stone (captain), half-backs; W. Bird, W. Dodsworth, C. Hill. S. Bradbury, W. Meek, H. Roberts, forwards. Stafford Road: Ray, goal; Durrance, Stanford, Jones, Richards, Gowland, Lane, Jackson, Baker, Daken, and C. Crump (captain).

WALSALL CUP.—ASTON UNITY v. SMALL HEATH ALLIANCE.—These clubs, being drawn together in the first round of the above competition, met at the Aston Lower Grounds on Saturday last. The Alliance played with the wind in the first half, but failed to score until about three minutes before half-time was called, when Arthur James by a tremendous long kick lowered the colours of the Unity. Upon change of ground, the home team forwards made several dangerous rushes on the Alliance goal, but the good play of Summers and Gessey at back, and Bodenham in goal, frustrated their efforts to score. The Alliance were more successful when playing against the wind, and after a good run on the left wing, Arthur James scored the second goal, off a splendid centre by Hards. Shortly before time was called, Rotherham was instrumental in adding another goal to the credit of the Alliance, after a capital bit of passing, and the match ended in favour of the visitors by three goals to none. Teams:—Unity: Goal, Mathews; back, Benson; half-backs, Lloyd, Upton, and Pallett; forwards, Coley, Rodgers, Heilborn, Ashford, Wilson, and Firmer. Alliance: Goal, Bodenham; back, Gessey; half-backs, T. James, Summers, and F. James; forwards, T. Whitehead, A. James, W. Slater, Teychenne, Hards, and Rotherham. Umpires, Messrs. Hundy and J. Harlow. Referee, Mr. Mason (Aston Villa).

STAFFORDSHIRE v. NORTH WALES.—A match was played at Stoke, on Saturday afternoon, between teams representing Staffordshire and North Wales. The weather was wretched, rain falling all the afternoon, often heavily, and a rough and gusty wind blowing.

Most games were classed as 'friendlies' and attractive games were played against clubs from even as far away as Scotland.

# FOOTBALL.

## WALSALL TOWN v. WALSALL SWIFTS.

### BIRMINGHAM AND DISTRICT CHALLENGE CUP
#### (FOURTH ROUND).

Seldom, perhaps, has a football match in Walsall caused so much excitement as did the game on Saturday last, between the above clubs. Both of them having shown such consistent form this season, and both having had such a run of successes, it was not to be wondered at that upwards of 4,000 spectators thronged the ropes. A pleasing feature was added to the game by the presence of a large number of ladies, who evinced the liveliest interest in the game, and heartily appreciated the efforts of the players in their keen struggle for supremacy. The weather was delightfully fine, the turf in very fair condition, and, as there was scarcely any wind, everything favoured a good match. Soon after the announced time the Swifts made their appearance on the Chuckery ground, and were soon followed by the visiting team. Both teams met with a hearty reception, and Dyoss, having won the toss, arranged his men with the hill against them, and Bradbury commenced the battle for the Town. The team at once attacked the home goal, Tapper and Yates being in the van; but Newman coolly returned the leather, and Bird, successfully tackling Brandrick, at once ran down to the Swifts' end, and Sheldon and Jones were now kept pretty busy for a time, Yates at length relieving his side. Taylor effectually stopped the rush by the opposing forwards, and once more the play was round the home goal, and Ashwell, being pressed by Bradbury and Bird, gave a corner. This was taken by Evans, who placed it nicely in front, and Roberts soon placed a goal to the credit of the Town, which was greeted with vociferous cheering. The home players did not seem to relish this, and at once commenced an exciting onslaught on the Town fortress, Farmer putting the ball well into goal, but Newman got it away. Yates next showed up prominently, and for a time the visitors were kept well in their own half. At this time there was a deal of unnecessary charging indulged in, much to the delight of the rougher element. Ashwell, Brandrick, Yates, and Sheldon put in some good work; and, after a corner by the Swifts had gone just the wrong side of the bar, Brandrick and Yates forced it over the Town line. The visitors next made a visit to the other end, but were brought back by the whistle. Tapper and Higgins showed up well, the latter especially, and a brilliant centre was nullified by none of the Swifts being up in time, Newman promptly putting it out of danger. Farmer and Brandrick both tried to lower the Town's colours, but to no purpose, and a very pretty run down the left by Dodsworth and Bird followed. Jones saved well, but Collington placed it neatly back, and then a foul by the Town relieved the home players, who were now being pressed. Farmer made a fine run into the Town quarters, and shot outside. Newman saved from a good rush by the Swifts, and Evans next gave a corner from a really splendid middle by Higgins. This was got away, and Bradbury took it down to the Swifts' goal, and Bird shot over the bar from a centre by the former. Stone made a good attempt to score, but Jones, with a clean kick, put it over the visitors' goal. A good chance was given to Brandrick by Yates, but was lost; and Tonks stopped a dangerous run by Brandrick and Farmer, and then the Swifts were in turn pressed. Dyoss and Higgins got well away, and a shot from Dyoss caused Keay to throw out. The ball now travelled at a rare pace from end to end, and a foul by the Town relieving the Swifts. A bad centre by Dodsworth spoilt a good

chance, and Brandrick and Lunn came away finely. Tonks gave a corner to save, and Yates put in a very smart shot, which looked like scoring, but Evans deliberately knocked it out with his hand, and Farmer came with a rush and put it through. An appeal from both teams was made, and the ball was eventually put down in front of goal, the result of the foul. This was got away by the Town players, and half-time arrived immediately after, the score standing at 1 to 0 in favour of the Town. A corner gained by the Swifts went outside, and Jones made a grand attempt to score. Yates next showed up remarkably well, as did also Collington and Taylor. Brandrick, Tapper, Farmer, Higgins, and Dyoss all put in excellent work; but Newman was playing in splendid form, and was invaluable to his side. Bradbury made a good attempt to get away, but Dyoss stopped him; and directly after a nice shot from Yates went straight into goal, Brandrick adding a little more force to it, and a loud cheer went up as the score was made equal. This was renewed immediately afterwards, as Farmer, Ashwell, and Brandrick got away at a rare pace, a fine attempt by the former striking the cross-bar, and, dropping in front, Brandrick shot it through. The Swifts now began to put the pace on, Tonks stopping a good rush. Higgins got a chance and shot, but Keay saved. The visitors made a pretty passing run up the field, Yates tackling brilliantly. Roberts had a rare chance to score, but missed his kick; and some effective close passing by Tapper and Dyoss was loudly cheered, and the former and Higgins visited the Town goal. The remaining portion of the game was intensely exciting, Farmer, Higgins, Yates, and Lunn attacking the visitors' goal repeatedly; whilst Newman, Jones, and Sheldon had plenty to do. A good run and score by Farmer was spoilt through a foul, and at the end of the game Jones had just saved well by heading out from a corner-kick. Although both sides tried hard no extra point was made, and the Swifts, therefore, were declared victors by two goals to one. At the termination of the game Dyoss, Yates, and Jones, amidst loud cheering, were carried off the field to the dressing tent. The following comprised the teams:—Town: Goal, Keay; backs, Newman (captain) and Tonks; half-backs, Collington, Taylor, and Evans; forwards, Roberts, Stone, Bradbury, Bird, and Dodsworth. Swifts: Goal, Hobson; back, Jones; three-quarter-back, Sheldon; half-backs, Dyoss (capt.), Yates, and Ashwell; forwards, Brandrick, Farmer, Lunn, Tapper, and Higgins. Umpires, Messrs. G. Bird and Dallard; referee, Mr. Crump (President of the above association).

---

## WALSALL ASSOCIATION v. WEDNESBURY CHARITY ASSOCIATION.

The first match organised by either of these local associations came off at the Swifts' ground, Walsall, on Monday afternoon. The weather was very fine, and about 1,600 were present. It is worthy of note that the chosen players turned up to a man, among them being several of our crack players. Walsall won the toss, and elected to play against the slope, and Wednesbury kicked off at 3.25. Walsall quickly showed to advantage, a couple of corners coming to nothing, while Farmer also had two unsuccessful shots. Wednesbury now pulled themselves together, and Roberts nearly scored; but just after the same player lowered the Walsall goal with a splendid low shot. Directly after Nicholls saved his goal well, and a rush of the Wednesbury forwards again scored. Even play followed, but then Roberts and Reeves kept Hubbard busy, and then Brandrick and Arblaster made a good run, and the former centring accurately to Bishton, he smartly did the needful. Upon

---

Not surprisingly, clashes between Town and Swifts were keenly contested and it's significant that on such occasions the local newspaper gave extra column inches to match reports.

From 1881 onwards both teams played at The Chuckery and one can only imagine the amount of noise generated when, as sometimes happened, both clubs were playing at home. On one remarkable day in November 1884 the Town side beat Willenhall 17-0 and the Swifts beat Nettlefolds Athletic 19-0. What a contrast to the early days when goals were so scarce. After over a decade of coexistence both the Town and the Swifts hit a bad patch and early in 1888 it was decided that the clubs should be amalgamated. This picture of Walsall Swifts is thought to date from 1881/82 when the Swifts won the Walsall Cup and the two teams played on adjacent pitches at the Chuckery ground.

Two early pictures of the new Walsall Town Swifts Club after the amalgamation of 1888. The colours were red and white striped shirts. Both pictures were probably taken at the old Chuckery Ground. Unfortunately, complaints from residents of the nearby Sutton Road led to Walsall Town Swifts having to leave the Chuckery in 1893 after just one season in the Second Division of the Football League.

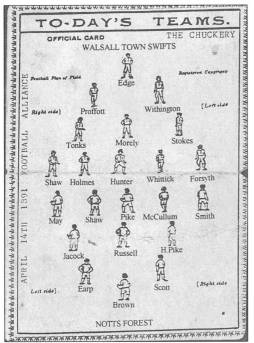

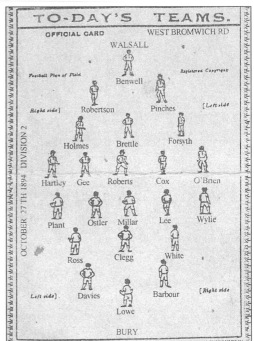

Early match cards (the forerunners of today's elaborate glossy programmes) reveal the diversity of games that had equal popularity in those days. Walsall played in the local Birmingham Senior Cup and the Staffordshire Cup as well as the Football League and the FA Cup, but still found time to put on a game against First Division neighbours Wolves for the benefit of the many unemployed in the area.

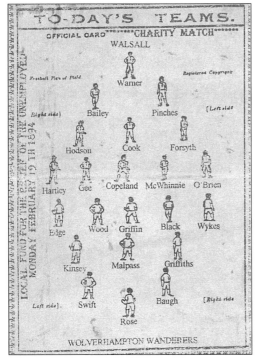

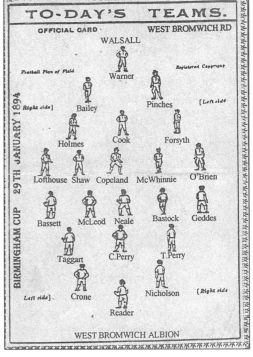

14

# SEASON 1893-4 SECOND DIVISION

T BROMWICH ROAD GROUND

T. HAWKINS

- BAILEY

R. SMELLIE

NOV: 11TH WALSALL v LIVERPOOL
1 (COX)    1 (BRADS)

- DAVIES    R. COOK    N. FORSYTH

S. HOLMES    - McWHINNIE    D. COPELAND    S. COX    T. O'BRIEN

In the first season at the new West Bromwich Road ground Walsall played a memorable game in Division Two against Liverpool that ended 1-1 in front of an estimated gate of 4,000. Though popular opinion held that this would become one of the top stadia in the area, Walsall moved away from West Bromwich Road after just three seasons when the new Hillary Street ground was opened in 1896.

15

NO. 39

~ WALSALL ~

# Football Club.

PRESIDENT    -    -    F. J. ZELLER, ESQ.

## Member's Ticket.

Admit to GROUND ONLY.
NOT available for English Cup Ties.

Mr. _Maltby_

G. HUGHES,

6/-                                    *Secretary*

A ground season ticket at the end of the last century. For six shillings a purchaser could see between fifteen and twenty League games. Has there ever been such value for money? We can accurately date this ticket from the fact that George Hughes was secretary for just one season, that of 1898/99.

Walsall officials seem to have taken a rather casual attitude toward losing their Football League status in 1901. Perhaps the fact that after dropping out in 1895 they had bounced back a year later had something to do with it.

**THE WALSALL OBSERVER AND SOUTH STAFFORDSHIRE CHRONICLE,**

**SATURDAY, AUGUST 3, 1901.**

### PEDESTRIANISM.

### LICHFIELD ATHLETIC CLUB
SPORTS.

### WALSALL FOOTBALL CLUB.

ELECTION OF OFFICERS.

### BROWNHILLS URBAN DISTRICT COUNCIL.

### LICHFIELD GRAMMAR SCHOOL
SPORTS.

This time, however, they had to wait twenty years before returning to the League as members of the new Division Three (North) in 1921.

17

No-one likes losing their place in the Football League and Walsall were no exception in 1901. The fact that they had secured 27 points from 34 games does seem to have given them some sort of case, particularly as just over fifty years later they survived in successive seasons with just 24 and 26 points respectively from 46 games. After some uncertainty during the close season, Walsall finally secured a place in the Midland League for the 1901/02 season. For all their troubles in surviving and despite winning only two of their first eleven Midland League games, Walsall managed to rally themselves in time to enjoy a spectacular FA Cup run, putting out Brierley Hill, Berwick, Port Vale and New Brompton (the original label for Gillingham) before chalking up a magnificent win over First Division Burnley. After just two seasons in the Midland League, Walsall moved into the Birmingham League where their most attractive opponents were Aston Villa Reserves. In 1909/10 Villa actually won their first eighteen games of the season, including the New Year's Day game when they beat Walsall 4-0.

Kirkham was firm, and, though the crowd hooted loudly, Cook had to go. For some time after this fouls were frequent, and much ill-temper was displayed. Fay went back, but he stayed there only a minute or two, and Oldham played the one-back game. Moreover, they severely taxed the Villa defence, till Hall, standing by himself well inside his own half, got the ball and started a brilliant run. He was not tackled till he reached the Oldham back; but Hamilton was not equal to the task of stopping him, and the Villa outside left ran round him, and gently placed the ball in goal out of the reach of Matthews. It was a superb individual effort—one of the very best we have seen this season. But Oldham were by no means done with, and, playing up with rare gallantry, Toward headed into the Villa net two minutes from the finish from a beautifully-placed centre by Broad. The Villa thus won by 2 goals to 1, and no one would deny they were the better side, sharper on the ball, and showing the finer football, though Oldham played a rare good Cup-tie game. Teams :—

OLDHAM ATHLETIC.—Matthews, goal; Cook and Hamilton, backs; Downie, Walders, and Wilson, half-backs; Broad, Fay, Toward, Montgomery, and Miller, forwards.

ASTON VILLA.—George, goal; Lyons and Miles, backs; Tranter, Buckley, and Hunter, half-backs; Wallace, Gerrish, Hampton, Bache, and Hall, forwards.

Referee: Mr. T. Kirkham (Burslem).

## Beaten at Last.

ASTON VILLA RESERVES LOSE AT WALSALL.

**Walsall 1, Aston Villa Res. 0.**

After going through nearly five months of the season without defeat, the Aston Villa Reserves were beaten at Walsall in their Birmingham League game. It was a keenly-contested match, marked by earnest, strenuous play on both sides; and, on the whole, a draw would have more correctly represented the run of the play—Walsall's goal (scored in the last few minutes) being the outcome of a misunderstanding between the Villa backs. When play had settled down, after the opening exchanges, Mann forced a corner, but this was cleared; and Walsall, getting away on the right, looked dangerous until a weak finish gave the Villa a chance—Walters shooting wide; and Mann,

when well placed, being given off-side. The home team played up in resolute fashion and gave the visiting defence an anxious time; but Layton and Kearns kicked and tackled well. Turner cleared a warm shot from Crump, and, when the ball was returned, the Villa goal had a rather lucky escape. The Walsall forwards were very quick on the ball, Davies and Dilly putting in some good work on the wings; and, with the halves playing good football, there was no end of excitement.

The interval arrived with nothing scored.

On resuming, the game was vigorously fought on both sides, and play was fairly even for some time. About seven minutes from the finish a misunderstanding by the Villa backs let the home side in, and Lyon scored the only goal of the match—the Villa Reserves thus sustaining their first defeat of the season. Teams :—

WALSALL.—Cooch, goal; Board and Chance, backs; Richards, G. Walker, and W. Walker, half-backs; Davies, Caddick, Lyon, Crump, and Dilly, forwards.

ASTON VILLA.—Turner, goal; Layton and Kearns, backs; Walker, Moss, and Kimberley, half-backs; Mann, Walters, Jones, Slater, and Henshall, forwards.

Referee: Mr. J. E. Sharpe (Lichfield).

## Our Portrait Gallery.

### F. MILES.

IT is with great pleasure that we reproduce a clever caricature of one of the most popular players that ever wore the Claret and Blue jersey—"Freddie" Miles. A clever and accomplished player, who never spares himself in the least, but goes the "whole hog," Miles has won his way into the affections of the Villa crowd alike by his abilities as a footballer, his sportsmanship on the field, and his gentlemanly bearing wherever he may be met. A generous opponent, he is fearless to a degree, and Villa interests are always felt to be safe when Freddie Miles is in the "last line." Miles has had a distinguished career, but has not always met with the recognition that was his due from the "powers that be." There is heaps of football in him yet, and we shall all wish him a long-continued welcome at Villa Park.

Just a fortnight later, however, Walsall won the return game and, as this report from the Villa programme indicates, became the first team to beat their famous neighbour's reserves that season.

19

Walsall had achieved some sort of consistency at this stage in their history, this team finishing fifth in the Birmingham League in 1909/10 behind Aston Villa Reserves, Crewe, Wolves Reserves and Brierley Hill. They also won the Walsall Senior Cup.

A season later they moved up to third place through the efforts of this team. Walsall again won the Walsall Senior Cup and were beaten in the final of the Staffordshire Senior Cup by Aston Villa. The familiar stripes on the front of the stand remained until well after the Second World War, changing from scarlet and white to claret and blue in 1920.

Walsall completed the 1914/15 season despite the fact that the First World War had broken out. In fact, in addition to winning the Walsall Senior Cup again they won the Keys Cup, which was awarded to the team finishing highest in the Birmingham League apart from the Reserve teams of local 'giants' Aston Villa, Birmingham, West Brom and Wolves.

## FOOTBALL.

### ENGLISH CUP.

### NOT THIS TIME.

**WALSALL'S PALACE JOURNEY
BROKEN AT SHREWSBURY.**

(By "REDBREAST.")

| | |
|---|---|
| Shrewsbury Town (h) | 2 |
| Walsall | 1 |

Walsall's exit from the English Cup competition not only came as a big disappointment, but it was made under most unsatisfactory circumstances. Had they been beaten after having put up a good fight no one could have grumbled, but unfortunately that was far from being the case. After the manner Walsall had disported themselves recently, more particularly in the previous stages of the competition, their display at Shrewsbury was quite a surprise. To go straight to the point, Walsall never really settled down to anything like decent football; there was absolutely no method in their play, and what was worse still they failed to take advantage of some glorious chances which presented themselves, the goal being missed on more than one occasion when it was merely a matter of shooting into the net. As a matter of fact, if Walsall had done what they ought to have done they would have had at least a couple of goals, if not three, during the first twenty minutes or so.

Walsall also achieved their longest-ever FA Cup run in that 1914/15 season, battling through no fewer than six rounds (defeating Willenhall, Cannock, Hednesford, Cradley Heath, Stoke and Wrexham) before going out to Shrewsbury with a very disappointing display.

# FOOTBALL CLUB.

## A SATISFACTORY SEASON CONSIDERING THE CIRCUMSTANCES.

## THE BOROUGH MEMBER AND THE FUTURE.

The annual meeting of the Walsall Football Club, which had been twice previously postponed, was fixed for Monday night at the "Hope and Anchor" Inn, Pleck, but owing to the meagre attendance—the Chairman (Mr. A. Medlam), the Secretary (Mr. Haydn Price), two committee men and three members—the business of the election of officers, &c., had to be again deferred.

The members of the Press, however, were supplied with a letter from the President (Sir Richard Cooper, M.P.) and the Secretary's report, for publication.

### Sir Richard Cooper's Opinion.

Sir Richard Cooper wrote:—

"I very much regret the difficulty I am placed in in attending your annual meeting. I should not regret this so much were it a fact that the club had passed through a prosperous season. At the same time a careful perusal of the balance sheet satisfies me that having regard to the very difficult circumstances under which the club has been compelled to work this past winter the result is eminently satisfactory and reflects great credit upon the administration of the club by the committee and by yourself as secretary. It has been a matter of some anxiety to me as your President whether the club should have continued its programme to the end of last season in view of the war, but having regard to the heavy financial obligations to which the club was committed and especially as football appeared to be singled out for attack, I felt that there was not sufficient reason for interfering with your programme and that football alone ought not to be stopped unless other similar forms of public amusement were similarly dealt with. I entirely endorse the decision of the Football Association as regards the past, but I do not hesitate to express the view that as the club is not now committed to heavy financial obligations for next season, and since the country realises that every ounce of effort has got to be put into the position of the war by those who are not in the Army, I do hold the opinion that League matches should not be arranged for the coming winter. I hope this will be the determination of the Football authorities, by whom, of course, the Walsall club must be principally guided."

In the circumstances it was perhaps not surprising that July 1915 saw the lowest-ever attendance at a Walsall FC annual meeting. Even so, the local MP, Sir Richard Cooper, who was club president, showed a determination to keep the flag flying as this report from the *Walsall Advertiser* of Saturday 10 July 1915 clearly shows. Walsall struggled on in 1915/16 playing in the local Walsall and District League, but as the war situation worsened they closed down until 1919.

# Two
# Between the Wars

Though Walsall had rather a lean time on the pitch in 1919/20, finishing in sixteenth place in the Birmingham League, they got together elaborate plans for the new 1920/21 season. The old scarlet jerseys were discontinued in favour of the claret and blue of their First Division neighbours Aston Villa and, with ex-army man Parr to lick them into shape as trainer and Joe Birchell to do the administrative work, the team looked ready for action. From left to right (players only), back row: W. Corbett, C. Wyke, J. Mackenzie. Middle row: E. Wilkins, H. Johnson, J. Kinsella. Front row: S. Ingram, T. Bowyer, E. Edwards, A. Groves, J. Mann, T. Rogers.

**Walsall**
# Football News

*The Official Programme of the Walsall Football Club.*

No. 14.    SATURDAY, JANUARY 1, 1921.    PRICE 2D.

**P**ARTIES desirous of
    booking a char-a-
    banc or private car
    for Walsall's away
    matches, should
    apply for terms to

## THE SPRINGHILL GARAGE,

*AUTOMOBILE AND MOTOR ENGINEERS,*

——— EALING HOUSE, ———

Upper Bridge St.,    -    -    WALSALL.

Telegrams : "Scooter" Walsall.    -    -    -    Telephones : 164 & 658.

Printed by the "Pioneer" Press, Lichfield Street, Walsall.

A new match programme was also launched. Up to then only single cards had been issued, but now an eight-page issue was made available to fans although, as today, the advertisement content was rather high.

Football News

## BOB PARSONS'
### SCHOOL OF BOXING AND PHYSICAL CULTURE,
ATHENÆUM  BUILDINGS,  BRIDGE  STREET,
WALSALL.

Looked upon by Experts as one of the most up-to-date Schools of Boxing in England.

### PRIVATE TUITION & MASSAGE BY APPOINTMENT.

#### Athletes Trained for their Engagements.

### TEAMS.

#### Wolverhampton Res.

Right | | | (12) GEORGE | | | Left
--- | --- | --- | --- | --- | --- | ---
| (13) NEWHILL | | | | (14) JONES |
(15) ROCKE | | | (16) CADDICK | | (17) WOODWARD |
(18) BIRD | (19) HALES | | (20) SAMBROOKE | | (21) LEARY | (22) LEA

Referee :—    O

(11) ROGERS    (10) BOWYER    (9) EDWARDS    (8) LANE    (7) INGRAM

(6) WILKINS    (5) GROVES    (4) KINSELLA

(3) McKENZIE    (2) CORBETT

Left    (1) J. HOUGHTON    Right

#### Walsall.

# OYSTERS
—— ARE ——
## NOW IN SEASON.

All our Oysters guaranteed PURE, from
Beds under Government inspection.

## .. Fresh Daily ..

# Oyster Rooms, H.M. Theatre Buildings.
F. HALL, Proprietor.

24

When the Third Division was extended to two sections in 1921, Walsall gained a place in the Northern Division and so returned to the Football League from whence they had been expelled twenty years earlier. Great excitement was generated in the town, a new stand was built on the Hillary Street ground and even for the public practice matches there was a gate of almost 6,000. After losing their opening game 1-0 at Lincoln, Walsall played their first home game in Division Three (North) on Saturday 3 September. They had the confidence to field an unchanged team and romped home 3-0 in front of a gate of 10,627 – how times had changed from that last home game in Division Two in 1901 when just 800 saw a goal-less draw with Middlesbrough.

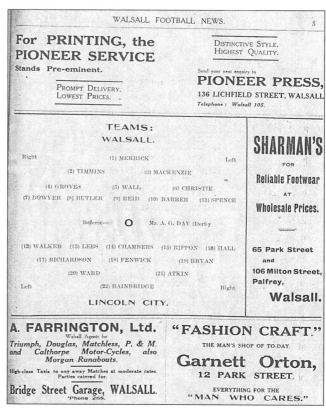

TEAMS:
WALSALL.

(1) MERRICK

Right                                                            Left

(2) TIMMINS                    (3) MACKENZIE

(4) GROVES          (5) WALL          (6) CHRISTIE

(7) BOWYER   (8) BUTLER   (9) REID   (10) BARBER   (11) SPENCE

Referee—    O    Mr. A. G. DAY (Derby)

(12) WALKER   (13) LEES   (14) CHAMBERS   (15) RIPPON   (16) HALL

(17) RICHARDSON          (18) FENWICK          (19) BRYAN

(20) WARD          (21) ATKIN

Left          (22) BAINBRIDGE          Right

LINCOLN CITY.

Walsall quickly settled into the new life in Division Three (North) and in only their second season finished in third place (at a time when only the top club went up). In fact, Walsall were just five points behind Nelson, who were promoted, and one behind Bradford Park Avenue, who just missed out. This was a typical line-up from that season. From left to right, back row: E. Langenove, H. Stanford. Middle row: B. Timmins, T. Bowen, E. Cameron, C. Harper, E. Groves. Front row: A. Groves, J. Walton, C. Cullum, G. Bradburn.

Remarkably, Walsall's biggest win in the successful 1922/23 season was in the last game – 5-0 against Division Three (North) champions Nelson. Another oddity is that although the average gate that season was 6,455, only 2,500 attended this final game; fans must have been disappointed at missing out on promotion.

In 1923 Walsall signed a goalkeeper who had played brilliant games against them in the Birmingham League days while with Darlaston. Harry Wait was already thirty-one years old when he made his Football League debut and kept a clean sheet in a 2-0 win at Rotherham. At one stage Harry played in 200 successive games and, although he retired at the age of forty in 1932, he came back four years later to help out in an emergency and, at the age of forty-four, conceded only five goals in five games. Later, Harry served the club for nearly twenty years as trainer and for ten more years after that as groundsman. Pictured above with his wife when in his eighties, Harry, who lived right opposite the ground in Wallows Lane, followed the club with interest right to the end of his life. Not surprisingly after a lifetime in football, Harry had a wealth of stories to tell in his latter days. Living as he did just opposite the ground, he was always available to people who dropped in at odd times. One day in 1935, he was approached by a small, fair-haired boy who asked him if he could have a trial, claiming that he was a goalkeeper. Just to oblige the lad, Harry took him into the ground and tried a few shots against him. Such was the boy's agility and safe handling that Harry immediately sought out the manager of the time, Andy Wilson. Harry's words were 'I think this lad's got a bit of an idea, Andy'. This proved to be something of an understatement as the boy was none other than Burt Williams, who made his first team debut at the age of seventeen, played for England in a wartime international while still with Walsall and, after moving to Wolverhampton Wanderers in 1945, went on to win 24 full caps, not to mention both FA Cup and League Championship winners' medals with Wolves.

THE WALSALL FOOTBALL NEWS

THE OFFICIAL PROGRAMME of the WALSALL FOOTBALL CLUB

SATURDAY JAN 8·1927.

J TORRANCE WALSALL

HOWARD BAKER CORINTHIANS

WALSALL v. CORINTHIANS

IN THE THIRD ROUND OF THE ENGLISH·F·A·CUP.

PRICE TWOPENCE

Walsall have become legendary for FA Cup giant-killing over the years, but they were the wrong side of a spectacular example in 1927 when the famous Corinthians amateur club won 4-0 at Hillary Street in a third round tie. The gate of 16,607 was the second highest at Hillary Street up to that point.

Roy John's career was one of the most remarkable that one could imagine. Signed from Swansea in 1928 as a left flank defender, he was tried as a goalkeeper in a reserve game and became the regular first team custodian within weeks. A year after getting into the Walsall first team he won the first of his 14 Welsh caps and, after moving to Stoke in 1932, went on to play for Preston, Sheffield United, Manchester United and Newport before retiring during the Second World War.

# )00 PEOPLE SEE ASTON VILLA'S
# P VICTORY OVER WALSALL

## ILLA PASS ON.

**·Fulfil Their Promise To Give First Leaguers A
·. Walker's Two Goals. Visitors' Second-Half
Rally, But — Class Will Tell.**

## DLESTONE THE HERO.

By "CRUSADER."

ing Walsall in the fourth
on Villa were called upon to
ager opposition of a Third
ean. They were old oppo-
competitive football, but the
rest centred in the neigh-
valry.

suffered a disappointment at
moment. It was found that
as not able to play owing to
d ankle. In his place John-
called upon. This was his
arance in the senior side this
Johnson was previously with
n and Crystal Palace.
vere unchanged, so that the
ed up as follows:—

ILLA.—Olney; Smart, Mort; Gibson,
s; York, Beresford, Brown, Walker,
res, Johnson

J. H. Whittle (Worcester).

olours of the clubs being
both changed, Villa appeared
and Walsall in blue.
welcome, cordial as it was,
o be exceeded in volume by
orded to Walsall, being
was renewed when Helliwell
toss and chose to defend the
urch end.
was quickly given off-side
ate pushed the ball to him.
Gibson intercepted with a
k.

R STARTS THE SCORING.

, however, were the first to
ose quarters, and Bradford put
irling shot which the wind
hang so that the first attempt

did not carry. Eyres tried a shot without, however, making any impression.
Villa's first attack brought success
after only four minutes' play.
WALKER took a subtle pass from Gibson and sent Houghton away, and from
the winger's centre Villa's captain
headed the ball direct into the net.
The goalkeeper had no chance of
reaching it.
Villa were on the warpath again in
the next minute, and Biddlestone did
well to gather a low centre from
Houghton before Brown could get to
it.
A plucky but ineffective spurt by
Walker was followed by a determined
solo thrust by Talbot, and it was left
to Houldey to check him by touching
the ball back to the goalkeeper when
the Villa centre-half had got through.
Then came an easy run and centre
by York, and Brown headed the ball
direct into Biddlestone's hands.

### WALSALL'S WAY.

Walsall relied largely upon hefty
volleys down the field, leaving the forwards to run after the ball in a spirit
of adventure, and when it was cleared
it generally happened that York or
Houghton had ample room in which to
operate. Biddlestone made a glorious
clearance from a centre which
Houghton was able to make from an
uncovered position.
Walsall had wretched luck in their
next attempt. A brilliant raid by the
forwards ending in Walters beating
Smart close in and firing in a great
drive which crashed against the
upright and rebounded.
Mason returned it but Olney gathered
it before it reached an opponent. This
attack gave Walsall encouragement

Itoe played a conspicuous part in some
movements which threatened more
than they accomplished, but, undoubtedly, worried Smart and Mort.
Left uncovered again, York made a
spirited advance from a model pass,
and when Brown and Biddlestone
kicked at the ball together the odds
were on a goal accruing, but luckily
for the Saddlers, the ball rose high in
the air and was cleared.
Excitement at vital moments cost
Walsall dearly. Eyres and Mason both
failed to gauge the strength of a pass
or the pace of the ball when Villa's
defence had been beaten by a series of
swift passes.

### VILLA PRESSURE.

Walters, moreover, sent the ball out
to Johnson when he might have well
ventured a shot.
Villa were deadly near goal, and
following a spurt in which York and
Houghton both loomed large Biddlestone gave a corner under difficulties
and then gathered a ticklish shot from
Walker.
Errors of judgment by Houldey and
Biddlestone presented the Villa with a
couple of corners. The defenders,
wrongly thinking that a goal kick
would accrue for letting the ball trickle
out when they could easily have
cleared; a third corner yielded Villa
their second goal after 25 minutes.
WALKER rushed in with a header
which Walters should have cleared
with ease, but the Walsall back missed
his kick, and the ball travelled into the
net.
Walsall made a plucky response to
this reverse, and Smart failing to check
a left wing raid, Eyres and Walters
got in a couple of shots, but neither of
them gave Olney any trouble.
The second clearance, in fact,
enabled Villa wingers to make a bold
advance marked by swinging passes
across the field, and York finished up
with a rasping shot which Biddlestone
did well to stop.
Weakness in finishing proved Walsall's undoing, for Mason had a golden
opportunity of improving matters
with a pass shrewdly provided by
Muldoon but he failed badly.
Houghton made much better use of
his chances, and it was from his telling work that Biddlestone made two
point-blank saves from Brown, who
spoilt his third chance by fouling a
defender.
In midfield there was not much to
choose but in front of goal Villa were

far more dangerous, and it was here
that the vital difference between
rivals lay.
Mort was a big factor in the Villa forwards and he twice intervened to good
purpose when the defence was spread.
Walsall's goal had some lucky es-
capes nearing the interval. Houldey
stopped a simple looking effort from
Gibson which would assuredly have
found the net, and Brown headed the
ball aside with Biddlestone out of his
goal.
There was one more thrill in the
Villa goalmouth and Olney was equally
lucky to get the ball away. Slowness
in shooting cost Walters another
chance but right on the interval JOHN-
SON scored for Walsall but the referee
yielded to Villa's protests to consult
the linesman before confirming his
original award.

Half-time:—Aston Villa ............... 2
Walsall ............... 1

There was a thrilling restart. Brown
burst through from a forward pass but
was stopped by Walters, whose name-
sake, inspired by the example and
shouldering Talbot out of the way,
finished up with a rasping drive just
wide of the mark.
This swift cut and thrust promised a
rousing second half. The succeeding
play confirmed it. Walsall were
tremendous triers, but commanding
just the vital little bit less of assurance
which seemed to carry Villa men along
so smoothly.
Houghton nearly snatched a goal out
of Helliwell's caution in trying to keep
the winger off the ball, but before the
attempt was cleared Biddlestone made
a couple of daring saves on his knees
only to see Beresford return the ball
to Walker, whose header missed the
goal by inches.

### BROUGHT "DOWN THE HOUSE."

This was followed by a characteristic
breakaway by Walsall, and Walters
was left with only the goalkeeper to
beat, but Olney advanced, and con-
trived to turn the ball behind for an
unproductive corner.
Walsall's spirit was magnificent,
and after Walters (T.) had brought
down the house with a wonderful overhead kick which held Brown to check
Houghton sent the ball right acress
goal for York to head wide in front of
an open goal.
Play continued while Walters lay
prone on the ground. Biddlestone distinguished himself by some fine saves
under difficulties before the ball went
into safety.

A little affair between Gibson
Roe brought a rebuke from the ref
This was followed by some brill
football by the Walsall left wing
it ended in Eyres testing Olney wi
glorious drive.
For a time Walsall were the m
aggressive, and their ardour in def
was only equalled by the swift
with which their forwards chas
attack into defence. A few seconds s
the referee had whistled for offs
Walters put the ball into the net,
the ruling was obviously the co
one.

### BIDDLESTONE THE HERO.

This warning alarmed the Villa
they retorted with real fire. Tate
missed the bar with a terrific d
and then Beresford failed badly
gift opening created by York.
In all these raids, Biddlestone pla
a heroic game and inspired
fullest confidence by his sure handling.

### WALSALL UNQUENCHABLE.

Walsall called heavily upon
factors—the genius of their goalke
and the unquenchable spirit of
whole team. The one defied Vill
the last gasp and the solid team w
offered them a sturdy challenge.
Villa's pressure became more inte
The attack was directed with skill a
each flank with the consequence
Walsall were confined to purely
fensive measures.
Although the Villa did not overc
their last resistance with ease,
kept their plucky opponents so
occupied that the few raids in w
the Saddlers were able to indulge w
desultory in character and did
seriously menace Olney's charge.
A keen raid by the Villa saw W
head the ball up against one po:
which it rebounded to the other
then rolled slowly to Houldey
exciting skirmish in front of Gt
who himself saved a difficult situa
by a dramatic thrust of his hand.
Two minutes from the end Bl
scored a simple goal for Villa. He
ton served with a pass which
centre-forward only just touche
convert into a goal.

Result:—Aston Villa ...................
Walsall .......................

### THE GAME AT A GLANCE.

After four minutes:—
Villa 1, Walsall 0.
(Walker scored.)
After 25 minutes:—
Aston Villa 2, Walsall 0.
(Walker scored.)
After 44 minutes:—
Aston Villa 2, Walsall 1.
(Johnson scored.)
After 88 minutes:—
Aston Villa 3, Walsall 1.
(Brown scored.)

The largest gate ever to watch a Walsall game was the 74,626 who were at Villa Park for a
fourth round FA Cup tie. Walsall had been drawn at home but the game was transferred to Villa
Park so that more fans could see the game. Men walked in their thousands from Walsall to
Birmingham and saw the Saddlers give a brave display before going down 3-1

Billy Bradford | Joe Johnson | Fred Walters | Albert Walters

Some of the players who battled bravely against Aston Villa in January 1930. Joe Johnson
scored the goal in what was his one and only first team game.

There was an interesting spin-off from Walsall's FA Cup game at Villa Park in 1930 in that just a month later their goalkeeper Fred Biddlestone, who had played an outstanding game, moved to Aston Villa. He went on to play a total of 160 games for Villa and during the war years made 70 guest appearances for Walsall.

A typical crowd scene from a Walsall home game during the 1930s. As can be seen in the picture, there was standing room in front of the main stand, white railings surrounded the pitch and an array of benches inside the railings accommodated the training staff and the band, which played before the game and at half-time.

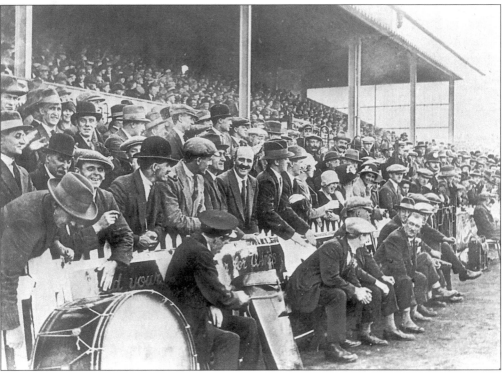

The front of the match programme for what turned out to be the greatest day in Walsall's history. This was when they beat Arsenal 2-0 in an FA Cup third round tie on 14 January 1933. Even a facsimile reprint of the match programme will command a £10 selling price these days and an 'original' will be well into three figures.

This was the team and officials for the greatest day in Walsall's history. From left to right, back row: S. Bird, J. Read, S. Bennett, H. Wait (trainer), J. Cunningham, E.G. Wilson (secretary), G. Leslie, H. Salt, W. Sheppard. Middle row: W.G. Slade (manager), E. Jackson (director), H.L. Fellows (chairman), Mayoress Mrs Dean, Mayor W. Dean, H. Lake (director), A.J. Eyre (director). Front row: W. Coward, C. Ball, G. Alsop, F. Lee.

**Sports Argus**

No. 1,817.    BIRMINGHAM, SATURDAY, 14 JANUARY, 1933.    ONE PENNY.

# GREAT CUP SENSATION:
# WALSALL BEAT ARSENAL

## WALSALL THE SURPRISE PACKET OF THIRD ROUND

**CUP EXIT OF THE MIGHTY ARSENAL**

**ALSOP & SHEPPARD**

**PLAYERS 'CHAIRED' BY SPECTATORS**

WALSALL to-day brought off one of the most sensational victories in the history of the F.A. Cup by their defeat of Arsenal, the League leaders.

The congratulations of the Midland football world go out to Walsall on their magnificent achievement.

The mighty Londoners failed to respond to goals scored in the second half by Alsop and Sheppard (penalty). Walsall played with zest and determination.

GILBERT ALSOP
(Walsall).

DESPITE the tremendous "draw" of the Arsenal, Walsall was far from being a London suburb this afternoon. In fact, the response from the capital was somewhat disappointing—trains being not nearly full, though motorcoaches were well loaded.

There was a minor trek from Birmingham, football "fans" normally at Villa Park transferring their affections for once. The ground was not filled to capacity, but extra precautions were taken to guard against a possible rush by those who had not purchased tickets.

The ground arrangements were admirable, and the extra police on gate duty were not needed.

Over an hour before the match about 2,000 people had assembled. The ground was soft and likely to cut up as the game progressed. Walsall "fans" claimed that this would suit their men.

Though Langford's absence from the Walsall eleven was regretted, the introduction of Salt, the former Brentford player, as left-half met with general approval.

There were few changes in the Arsenal side—Warne for Hulme; Sidey for John, and Walsh, a young London boy out of the second team, for Lambert. Teams:

WALSALL—Cunningham; Bennett, Bird; Reed, Leslie, Salt; Coward, Ball, Alsop, Sheppard, Lee.
ARSENAL—Moss; Male, Black; Hill, Roberts, Sidey; Warne, Jack, Walsh, James, Bastin.
Referee: Mr. A. Taylor (Wigan).

There were about 16,900 spectators when the game started. Red-led Walsall in blue and white stripes, on the field closely followed by Arsenal in white jerseys.

Walsall won the toss and kicked down the slope.

### EARLY WALSALL RAIDS

Coward went off at once on Walsall's right, but his progress was soon checked. Ball got possession, and Arsenal were strongly pressed in the first few minutes.

Moss ran out, but Black cleared before the goalkeeper could get to the ball.

Alsop made a capital attempt to break through, but was stopped by Male.

Then a clever run by Coward enabled him to put across goal, and Lee looked like scoring but his header was splendidly stopped by Moss.

Alsop got clean through for Walsall after seven minutes, but Moss turned the ball outside.

### ARSENAL IN PICTURE

The home side were having the better of the encounter, and when Lee dashed in from the left and shot Moss had to drop on the ball. He was quickly surrounded but the game was stopped for a foul.

Arsenal were then able to get away and Cunningham stopped a hot long shot from James.

To stem another attack Bennett put the ball outside.

Once when a foul was given against Walsall there were cries of disapproval. Arsenal's forwards were very smart, and it was only with difficulty that Bird stopped a fine rush from the right wing.

There was again disapproval when Ball was penalised.

Arsenal played with greater cohesion and speed, but the Walsall players bustled them off the ball.

Leslie was a splendid tackler for Walsall and pulled up two or three rushes.

The next movement saw Alsop and Coward cleverly work the ball along the right wing but the Arsenal backs were not shaken.

Bastin got an opening and rushed close in but Cunningham brought off a clever clearance.

Walsall were not long before they were again close in but Sidey relieved when the defence was hard pressed by Coward.

Walsall had an escape when Bastin centred across the goal and Jack just missed with a header.

Lee was afterwards fouled and a warm scrimmage near Arsenal's goal ended in Ball shooting over the bar.

Walsall continued to hold their own. Just before the interval the game was temporarily stopped while Hill received attention.

Alsop put in a lovely drive, but Moss cleared.

Half-time:—Walsall ........ 0
Arsenal ........ 0

### NOT STANDING ON CEREMONY

Arsenal attacked on the resumption and forced a corner, but nothing came of it. Warnes threatened danger, but Bird successfully tackled him.

Walsall were pressed for some time and had a narrow escape when Bastin put across goal and Walsh just missed the post by inches.

It was vigorous football and Arsenal were kept off their smart passing by first-time tackling.

From a breakaway Coward threatened Arsenal's defence but Black was equal to the occasion.

Once Sheppard tried to dribble through and was brought down outside the penalty area. A free-kick led to exciting work in Arsenal's goal but it had no result.

Rushing to the other end James tried a shot which missed the bar, Cunningham also kicked over the bar a difficult high shot from Bastin.

After 15 minutes' play this half Walsall scored.

The ball was headed through by ALSOP from near the corner of the post.

Sidey was limping and although Arsenal played with renewed ardour after the goal against them Leslie pulled them up on two occasions.

Then a very exciting incident happened for Alsop was brought down in the penalty area and an Arsenal defender was cautioned.

A penalty was allowed, from which SHEPPARD scored a second goal for Walsall.

It was a fierce encounter, and a free-kick against Walsall, just outside the penalty line, was dangerous, but Arsenal only managed to shoot outside.

Arsenal were trying desperately, and Leslie just managed to stop one of the Arsenal's forwards who was nearly through.

contd on next sheet.

An evening sports paper conveys the news of the sensation to the whole of the West Midlands.

Gilbert Alsop not only scored the opening goal in the game against Arsenal in 1933, but in two separate spells with Walsall netted 169 goals in 222 games plus another 56 in 100 wartime games. Here, he dives to head home in typical fashion. Alsop retired from first team football in 1947 soon after playing in an FA Cup tie against Liverpool and then had a spell as third team player-coach. He later returned to serve the club as groundsman and attended games right up to the end of his life. He died in 1992, but his name is still alive as fans sit in the Gilbert Alsop stand at the Bescot Stadium.

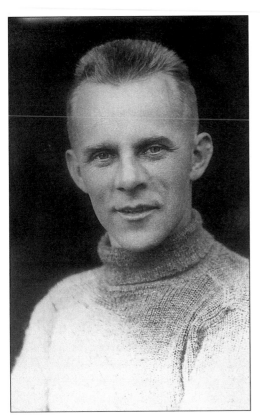

Walsall have rarely been short of a good goalkeeper and in pre-war days they were rarely short of a former Coventry City player. Scotsman Peter McSevich came into both categories, moving to Walsall in 1933 from Highfield Road and missing only a handful of games before injury ended his career three years later. He went on to serve the club as goalkeeping coach and dressing room attendant, living in Dickenson Drive just a few yards from the ground until his death in 1982.

This autograph sheet from the 1935/36 indicates just how quick a turnover of players there was at the time, since only defender Jack Bennett and midfielder Johnny Reed had survived from the team that beat Arsenal in 1933. This was the season in which Bill Evans, a signing from Cannock Chase Colliery, scored 24 goals in 34 League games.

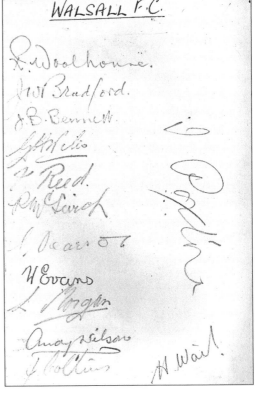

One of the legendary names in Walsall's history is that of H.L. Fellows. He became a director when the club became a limited company on rejoining the Football League in 1921. He took over as chairman in 1926. Fellows' devotion to the club was recognised in 1930 when the Hillary Street ground was renamed Fellows Park. His greatest moment as chairman came when Walsall beat Arsenal in 1933. Lawrence Fellows' devotion to the club is indicated by his Will. Written just a few hours before his death in 1938, it foregoes what was then a massive sum of £2,000 which the club owed to him.

Because of their geographical position, Walsall were one of the teams that moved between the northern and southern sections of Division Three in order to balance the numbers. One of these adjustments was made in 1936 and this is the squad that played in Division Three (South) in the club's first season there since 1931. From left to right, back row: J. Bewick, J. Bradford, L. Morgan, J. Shelton, H. Wait (trainer), J. Leckie, J. Bennett, N. Smith, J. Reed, G. Wiles. Middle row: L. Dunderdale, T. Jones, I. Harwood, Andy Wilson (manager), E. Wilson (secretary), R. Woolhouse, C. Bulger, J. Landells. Front row: G. Cunningham, J. Green, K. Harper, H. Dover, W. Evans, J. Bell, W. Richmond.

This is the Walsall staff which began the last pre-war season of 1938/39. They lost their first five games and did not chalk up their first win until November. However, they ended the season in style with 27 goals in six games, Gilbert Alsop getting 17 of them after being re-signed from Ipswich Town. Unfortunately, the deficit was just too great to make up and they had to seek re-election.

# THE FOOTBALL LEAGUE, SEASON 1938-39

## THIRD DIVISION (Southern Section)

Date of Match _Sept 5th_ 1938

Home Club _Cardiff City_    Visiting Club _Walsall_

Result :—Home Club _2_ Goals ; Visiting Club _1_ Goals.

Total No. of Matches Played _4_

Won _0_    Lost _4_    Drawn _0_

Total Goals for _3_ Against _8_ Points _0_

Signed _Ernest Wilson_    Secretary of _Walsall_ Club

---

## TEAM.

*Note.—The Surname, with Full Initials, must be given.*

|  |  |
|---|---|
| Goal | Lewkesbury K.C. |
| Backs (Right) | Beeson G. |
| " (Left) | Male N A. |
| Half-Backs (Right) | Godfrey C. |
| " (Centre) | Morgan H.B. |
| " (Left) | Simpson W.S. |
| Forwards (Outside Right) | Davies B. |
| " (Inside Right) | Evans W. |
| " (Centre) | Bambrick J. |
| " (Inside Left) | Hill J. |
| " (Outside Left) | Ledwood B. J. |

Advertised Time of Kick-off _6-15 p.m._    Actual Time of Kick-off _6-15 p.m._

## REPORT ON OFFICIALS

So that the Management Committee can keep an accurate record of the value of each Referee's work will you please insert in your Report the index figure which in your opinion most fairly assesses the value of his work.

| Index Figure 0 indicates Bad, Incompetent. |
|---|
| " " 1 " Poor. |
| " " 2 " Fair Average. |
| " " 3 " Satisfactory. |
| " " 4 " Very Good |

Date of Match _5th Sept_ 1938

Home Club _Cardiff City_    Visiting Club _Walsall_

Result : Home Club _2_ Goals ; Visiting Club _1_ Goals

Referee _W. T. Stringel_    Index Figure _2_

Comments (if any)

Linesman _A. B. Baughan_

Comments (if any)

Linesman _A. B. Alsop_

Comments (if any)

Signed _Ernest Wilson_    Club _Walsall_

A typical team sheet from pre-war days. Of the eleven who played in this game at Cardiff in the last pre-war season, only left-back Norman Male was still playing eight years later when normal League football resumed after the war.

## Huddersfield Town

Goal

Kick-off 3-0 p.m.          1 **Hesford**

Backs

2 **Hayes**                        3 **Mountford**

Half-Backs

4 **Willingham**          5 **Young**                    6 **Boot**

Forwards

7 **Isaac**        8 **Barclay**      9 **Price**      10 **McCall**      11 **Beasley**

Referee—
T. BENTLEY (Manchester).

Linesmen—
H. HARTLES (Red Stripe).
H. TRENHOLM (Blue Stripe).

12 **Bulger**      13 **Simpson**      14 **Bambrick**      15 **Alsop**      16 **Hancocks**

Forwards

17 **Payne**                    18 **Morgan**                    19 **Woodward**

Half-Backs

20 **Male**                              21 **Beeson**

Backs

22 **Tewkesbury**

Goal

## Walsall

Colours : Claret and Blue Shirts, White Knickers.

Despite their unhappy season in Division Three (South) in 1938/39, Walsall reached the last sixteen of the FA Cup for the first time ever, beating Carlisle, Clapton Orient, Newport County and Notts County en route and putting on a brave display in the fifth round before going down 3-0 at Leeds Road in front of a crowd of 33,543.

It was one of the ironies that, after having to seek re-election in the previous two seasons, Walsall seemed to have collected together a side likely to do well in 1939/40, only for the Second World War to destroy their ambitions alongside those of millions of people. With a new kit of claret and blue hoops (as opposed to the claret with blue sleeves) they held a most successful public practice match with the hopes of 4,515 fans running high.

To celebrate the diamond jubilee of the Football League, each Football League team played a pre-season game against neighbouring opponents and Walsall again walked tall against Mansfield Town. Oddly enough the Mansfield goal was scored by Bill Moore, who just over twenty years later was to manage Walsall as they climbed from Division Four to Division Two in two seasons.

## Dai Richards Shines at Fellows Park

WALSALL had seven new players in the public practice match at Fellows Park to-day.

Bambrick, who was re-signed after being put on the transfer list, did not turn out owing to throat trouble.

BLUES.—Strong; Beeson. Male; Richards. Morgan, Godfrey; Taylor, Adams, Beasley, Brown Gore.

CLARET AND BLUES. — Williams; Harper, Jones; Newman, Thayne, Payne; Hancocks, Shelton. Alsop, Talbot. Bulger.

Referee: B. W. Hutchins.

After 10 minutes' play the Claret and Blues went ahead. Talbot put out a nice pass to Hancocks, who centred for ALSOP to score with a low shot.

Play was fast in the early stages, but there was little incident.

Blues did much of the attacking for a time and Dai Richards, at right-half, and Taylor, the new outside-right from Notts County, were prominent. The forward line as a whole worked smoothly.

The Claret and Blues, however, whose forward line consisted of the probable League side players, were more polished and Talbot quickly

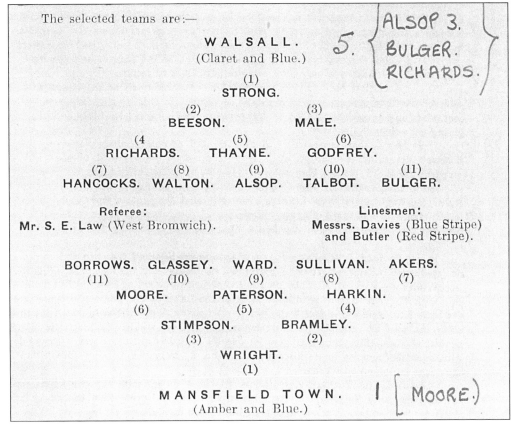

The selected teams are:—

**WALSALL.**
(Claret and Blue.)

*5.* ALSOP 3.
BULGER.
RICHARDS.

(1)
STRONG.

(2)　　　　　　　(3)
BEESON.　　　　　MALE.

(4　　　　(5)　　　　(6)
RICHARDS.　THAYNE.　GODFREY.

(7)　　　(8)　　　(9)　　　(10)　　　(11)
HANCOCKS.　WALTON.　ALSOP.　TALBOT.　BULGER.

Referee:　　　　　　　　　　　Linesmen:
Mr. S. E. Law (West Bromwich).　　Messrs. Davies (Blue Stripe)
　　　　　　　　　　　　　　　and Butler (Red Stripe).

BORROWS.　GLASSEY.　WARD.　SULLIVAN.　AKERS.
(11)　　　(10)　　　(9)　　　(8)　　　(7)

MOORE.　　　PATERSON.　　HARKIN.
(6)　　　　　(5)　　　　(4)

STIMPSON.　　　BRAMLEY.
(3)　　　　　(2)

WRIGHT.
(1)

**MANSFIELD TOWN.**　　　*1* MOORE.)
(Amber and Blue.)

One of many players who lost his last few seasons as a player to the Second World War was Irish international Joe Bambrick. This well-built striker was thirty when he moved to Walsall from Chelsea in 1938. He got 20 goals in 41 League and Cup games in 1938/39 but he returned to Ireland when war broke out and his playing days were over by the time peace returned in 1945.

# *Three*

# The War Years

For a few weeks, clubs continued to produce eight-page programmes for wartime games but paper shortages soon reduced them to single sheets. This one, for a Birmingham *v.* Walsall regional game, is full of interest with R.E. Foulkes, who was in the Blues side that day, joining Walsall at the end of the war and becoming an outstanding central defender, while in the Walsall side were two Aston Villa players, George Edwards and Ronnie Starling, making guest appearances.

# FOOTBALL FINIS—PRO TEM

## Saddlers Hard Fight To Defeat Queens Park Rangers

### BULGER NETS WINNER

## A Large Crowd Forgot Troubles For Couple Of Hours

WELL, despite all our hopes and wishes, war has come and football must go (writes " The Swift "). At least for the time being the roar of guns and aeroplane engines cannot be mixed with that of the goal-hungry crowd; but I think that once the country has settled down to war-time behaviour the authorities will allow soccer again in the provinces. There is nothing like a keen football match to make the timidest man forget his worries and troubles.

It was definitely so on Saturday at Fellows Park. Although the crowd obviously realised that the position was deadly serious and it was only a matter of minutes or a miracle before they would be involved in the bloody business of war, for two hours they had thoughts for nothing else than the Walsall—Queen's Park Rangers' game.

And the 8584 spectators who witnessed the game and saw Walsall register an orphan goal victory will remember it not only as the last of the pre-war games but also for the tremendous interest in the match.

Queen's Park have always been tough opponents and in latter years have almost always gone away with both points tucked snugly away in their travelling trunks. There was no falling away in their zest on Saturday, but a first-minute goal from Bulger could not be nullified against a device which was giving nothing away.

To Bulger must go our congratulations for scoring that goal, but to him Harper goes the biggest bouquet for his marvellous display at right back in place of the injured Beeson. Never putting a foot wrong, nor making an ineffective tackle, Harper alone at times stood between the Rangers forwards and Strong—and always he won.

An injury to Alsop in the first half rather handicapped the Walsall attack but one could not help but feel that the inside men should again have taken on more the role of attackers than defenders. Thayne showed convincingly that he needs no help blotting out centre forwards, and when football again comes to Fellows Park, let us hope that attack will again be the predominant factor of the line.

Queen's Park attacking downhill, were soon away, but after Fitzgerald had shot wide, Walsall got moving and scored in two minutes.

Richards released the pressure with a big cross kick to Bulger, who raced in and hooked the ball across goal.

Jefferson cleared, but Talbot secured and swung the ball over to Hancocks, who centred first time, and Bulger ran in and netted easily from close range.

Walsall continued to attack and the Rangers goal had a narrow escape from another Hancocks centre.

For some time the Rangers were clearly rattled and their defence was hard worked to prevent a further score.

A long pass downfield saw Mangnall make a great dash, but Harper beat him to the ball and cleared with a big kick.

Again Harper came to the rescue when Mangnall showed his paces, and then Walsall again took up the attack.

Talbot and Bulger worked through, but Reay intervened just in time.

Alsop was hurt in a collision with Allen and had to receive attention.

Fitzgerald was penalised for a foul on Male, and from the kick Hancocks had the Rangers' defence in trouble again with a clever move.

Jefferson cleared under difficulties, but again Walsall got moving, and Allen had to save a low drive by Walton.

He succeeded in scooping the ball out from the foot of the post.

Rangers occasionally showed flashes of good work, but Stock was being sadly neglected and rarely got a look at the ball.

When he was brought into the game he engineered a dangerous move but Swinfen ran into an offside position.

Walsall were soon back, and a Walton-Hancocks-Richards movement had the Rangers defence on the run.

Hancocks worked through to deliver another fine centre. Reay partially cleared, but Bulger secured and shot a yard wide.

Stock was again to the fore and Mangnall got his head to a centre to turn the ball well wide.

For some time Rangers played extremely well, and Harper and Male were kept hard at it, but apart from a lob by Swinfen, Strong was not seriously troubled.

A sharp raid on the left saw Fitzgerald get the better of Richards and Harper and centre the ball across goal, but no one could reach it.

Rangers could not be shaken off and from a free kick Strong had to fist away from Lowe.

Walsall were having their work cut out to prevent an equaliser, but they packed well under pressure.

Towards half-time Walsall attacked again and Hancocks showed up cleverly.

Walsall nearly went further ahead for the first run down, Talbot racing in to secure a pass. From his centre Bulger headed against the angle of the bar, with Allen beaten.

A minute later Talbot worked his way in to deliver a low drive which Allen had difficulty in holding.

Rangers hit back and Fitzgerald drove in hard, but wide.

Male and Godfrey were kept hard at work for some minutes, but Walsall hit back, and loud cries for a penalty against Jefferson were waved aside by the referee.

Rangers were kept defending for a long stretch, but Alsop was evidently feeling the effects of his early injury, and was not as troublesome as usual.

Hancocks was injured in a tackle and had to receive attention.

Again Rangers attacked, and Thayne conceded a corner to check Swinfen.

An equaliser looked like coming when Bonass rounded Harper, but the winger's centre travelled across the goalmouth without a player being to reach it.

Mangnall finished up in the net in this effort. The Walsall attack got a little ragged for a time, but was still able to worry the Rangers, Walton driving a yard over with a great shot.

Rangers were fighting for all they were worth, and Bonass and Fitzgerald caused Harper anxiety but he stuck to his task. Mangnall was next in the wars following a goalmine tussle.

After attention, Mangnall was able to resume and he almost scored at once, Swinfen broke through and from his pass Mangnall shot just over the angle of the bar.

Hancocks was again prominent with a centre after beating Lowe and Reay, but Rudyard's height beat Alsop.

The teams were as follow:

**WALSALL**—Strong; Harper, Male; Richards, Thayne Godfrey, Hancocks, Walton, Alsop, Talbot, Bulger.

**QUEEN'S PARK RANGERS**—Allen; Reay, Jefferson; Lowe, Rudyard, Farmer; Stock, Swinfen, Mangnall, Fitzgerald, Bonass.

Referee: G. L. Iliffe (Leicester).

## LEAGUE TABLES AND RESULTS

### FOOTBALL

#### DIVISION I

| | | |
|---|---|---|
| Blackpool | 2 | Wolves ... 1 |
| Derby County | 1 | Aston Villa ... 0 |

#### DIVISION II

| | | |
|---|---|---|
| Birmingham | 1 | Burnley ... 0 |
| West Brom. A. | 3 | Tottenham H. ... 4 |

#### DIVISION III (Southern Section)

| | | |
|---|---|---|
| Walsall | 1 | Queen's Park R. ... 0 |

LEAGUE TABLE.

| | P. | W. | L. | D. | for | ag. | P. |
|---|---|---|---|---|---|---|---|
| Reading | 3 | 2 | 0 | 1 | 6 | 3 | 5 |
| Exeter City | 3 | 2 | 0 | 1 | 5 | 3 | 5 |
| Notts County | 2 | 2 | 0 | 0 | 6 | 2 | 4 |
| Ipswich Town | 2 | 2 | 0 | 0 | 5 | 3 | 4 |
| Brighton | 3 | 2 | 1 | 0 | 4 | 3 | 4 |
| Cardiff City | 3 | 2 | 1 | 0 | 6 | 4 | 4 |
| Crystal Palace | 3 | 2 | 1 | 0 | 9 | 4 | 4 |
| Bournemouth | 3 | 1 | 1 | 1 | 13 | 4 | 3 |
| WALSALL | 3 | 1 | 1 | 1 | 4 | 3 | 3 |
| Southend United | 3 | 1 | 1 | 1 | 4 | 3 | 3 |
| Clapton Orient | 3 | 0 | 0 | 1 | 1 | 4 | 3 |
| Norwich City | 3 | 1 | 1 | 1 | 4 | 4 | 3 |
| Torquay United | 3 | 0 | 0 | 3 | 4 | 4 | 7 |
| Bristol City | 3 | 1 | 1 | 1 | 5 | 5 | 3 |
| Mansfield Town | 3 | 1 | 1 | 1 | 5 | 5 | 3 |
| Queen's Park Rangers | 3 | 0 | 1 | 2 | 4 | 5 | 2 |
| Watford | 3 | 0 | 1 | 2 | 4 | 6 | 2 |
| Northampton | 3 | 0 | 2 | 1 | 4 | 6 | 2 |
| Port Vale | 2 | 0 | 1 | 1 | 0 | 1 | 1 |
| Swindon Town | 3 | 0 | 2 | 1 | 5 | 4 | 1 |
| Aldershot Town | 3 | 0 | 2 | 1 | 2 | 5 | 1 |
| Bristol Rovers | 3 | 0 | 2 | 1 | 2 | 7 | 1 |

## THE A.F.A. SUSPEND ACTIVITIES

### But Walsall Clubs Can Play Friendly Matches

An emergency meeting of the Birmingham and District Amateur Football Association decided on Tuesday night to suspend activities until the normal life of the nation is resumed.

Arrangements had been made to open the season in a fortnight.

It was stated that some grounds had been taken over for training purposes and that most of the association officials and many of the players would be fully occupied in National Service.

The hope was expressed that some clubs might find themselves in a position to arrange friendly games but this was entirely for the individual clubs themselves to decide.

Local teams competing in this association are Walsall Jolly Club, Walsall Phoenix, Walsall Naigo, Walsall Trinity and Wednesbury Amateurs.

The Walsall Senior League have postponed Saturday's fixtures and are in communication with the Walsall F.A.

---

2 September 1939 was a bittersweet day for Walsall fans as 8,584 were present at Fellows Park to see Walsall beat QPR 1-0 with Charlie Bulger getting the match-winner in the second minute. War was declared a few hours later and, of the team that played that day, only Norman Male, Gilbert Alsop and Les Talbot were with the club after the war, although Jim Strong went on to play many times for Burnley, Ken Harper played a few games for Barnsley and Johnny Hancocks won international honours while with Wolves.

Some remarkable scorelines were chalked up during the war years, none more so than an 11-4 win over Notts County on 9 November 1940. Just a fortnight earlier they had drawn 6-6 with Mansfield, but sadly at that time of great national danger only 427 fans were present. Striker Jack Vinall netted a hat-trick in the remarkable Notts County game. This former Sunderland and Norwich striker was actually on the books of Luton at the time and was guesting with Walsall. He signed for Walsall at the end of the war, but at the age of thirty-five played just two games in midfield when League football was resumed.

Through the ups and downs of wartime football, defender Jack Shelton brought a measure of consistency by playing in a total of 193 games. He was the son of Jack Shelton senior, who had played in Wolves' 1908 FA Cup-winning team.

One of the most remarkable rallies of all time was that of Walsall in a wartime game against a star-studded Aston Villa team on 2 October 1943. Losing 4-0 at the interval, they battled back to draw 4-4 and almost got a last-minute winner.

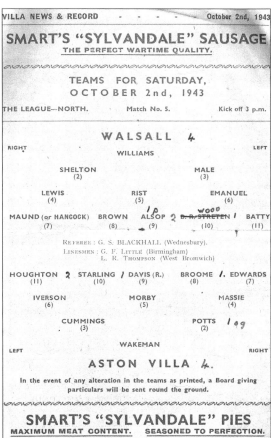

Starring in that remarkable 4-4 draw was skilful winger Jackie Maund, who had been an Aston Villa pre-war star. He guested for Walsall during the war, joined them immediately afterwards and, after retiring as a player in 1948, was on their training staff until 1957.

# Fellows Park News

### AND OFFICIAL PROGRAMME

No. 3     *Price One Penny*     25TH SEPTEMBER, 1943

## WALSALL

Colours—Claret and Blue Hooped Shirts, Black Knickers.

Right             WILLIAMS             Left

SHELTON (2)       RIST (5)       MALE (3)       WOOD (6)

LEWIS (4)

NICHOLLS (7)     BROWN (8)     ALLSOP (9)     B. R. STRETEN (10)     BATTY (11)

HOUGHTON (11)     STARLING (10)     BROOME (9)     HAYCOCK (8)     EDWARDS (7)

IVERSON (6)       MORBY (5)       MASSIE (4)

CUMMINGS or GODFREY (3)       POTTS (2)

Left             WAKEMAN             Right

## ASTON VILLA

Colours—Shirts : White ; Knickers : White.

Referee : Mr. J. T. DAVIS (Walsall)

Linesmen : Messrs. P. HARVEY and A. H. TOLLEY

### FOOTBALL LEAGUE NORTH REGIONAL FIXTURES—1943-4.

| 1943 | | | GOALS FOR | AGST | 1943 | | | GOALS FOR | AGST |
|---|---|---|---|---|---|---|---|---|---|
| Aug. 28 | Northampton Town | Away | 0 | 2 | Dec. 11 | Coventry City | Home | | |
| Sep. 4 | Northampton Town | Home | 0 | 0 | ,, 18 | Stoke City | Home | | |
| ,, 11 | Coventry City | Away | 3 | 3 | ,, 25 | Stoke City | Away | | |
| ,, 18 | Coventry City | Home | 1 | 1 | ,, 27 | Coventry City | Away | | |
| ,, 25 | Aston Villa | Home | | | **1944** | | | | |
| Oct. 2 | Aston Villa | Away | | | Jan. 1 | Coventry City | Home | | |
| ,, 9 | Northampton Town | Away | | | ,, 8 | West Bromwich Albion | Home | | |
| ,, 16 | Northampton Town | Home | | | ,, 15 | West Bromwich Albion | Away | | |
| ,, 23 | Wolverhampton Wand. | Home | | | ,, 22 | Northampton Town | Home | | |
| ,, 30 | Wolverhampton Wand. | Away | | | ,, 29 | Northampton Town | Away | | |
| Nov. 6 | Birmingham | Home | | | Feb. 5 | Stoke City | Away | | |
| ,, 13 | Birmingham | Away | | | ,, 12 | Stoke City | Home | | |
| ,, 20 | West Bromwich Albion | Home | | | ,, 19 | Wolverhampton Wand. | Home | | |
| ,, 27 | West Bromwich Albion | Away | | | ,, 26 | Wolverhampton Wand. | Away | | |
| Dec. 4 | Coventry City | Away | | | | | | | |

**Next Home Match, 16th October : NORTHAMPTON TOWN.**     **Kick-off 3 p.m.**

This rather battered wartime programme records the remarkable situation when two future England international goalkeepers were in the Walsall team beaten 2-0 by Aston Villa. Bert Williams, who went on to play for Wolves and England, was in goal while Bernard Streten, who was capped by England as a goalkeeper in 1950 while with Luton Town, was playing up front.

# Four
# The Post-war Years

After the end of the Second World War in May 1945, football experienced a transitional season in 1945/46, with the FA Cup being contested on a normal basis but the Football League still functioning regionally. Walsall competed in what was the northern section of Division Three (South). In the course of the season, new manager Harry Hibbs, the former Birmingham City goalkeeper, got together what many consider to be one of the finest teams ever to represent Walsall FC. This photograph is of a typical 1945/46 line-up. From left to right, back row: H. Wait (trainer), R. Crutchley, I. Methley, J. Lewis, N. Male, A. Newman. Front row: J. Hancocks, A. Mullard, D. Wilshaw, L. Talbot, A. Evans, R. Foulkes.

**CHELSEA FOOTBALL & ATHLETIC CO. LTD.**

# Official Programme

Directors:— J. H. MEARS (Chairman), J. E. C. BUDD,
C. I. PRATT, H. J. M. BOYER, L. J. MEARS.
Manager-Secy. :—Wm. BIRRELL.
Ground :—STAMFORD BRIDGE, S.W.6. 'Phone :—FUL. 3321.

| Saturday, May 4th, 1946. | Price Twopence |
|---|---|

## SOUTH CUP FINAL

# BOURNEMOUTH v. WALSALL

## Saturday, May 4th, 1946
Kick off 3 p.m.

### THEY FIGHT FOR THE CUP TODAY
By JOHN GRAYDON
*Special Writer " Sporting Chronicle and Athletic News "*

Walsall and Bournemouth, who today meet in the Final of the League South Cup, are both clubs with a wealth of experience behind them.

Take Walsall for instance. It was way back in 1892, when they were known as Walsall Town Swifts—a title they dropped for plain Walsall after a couple of seasons—that the Midland club left junior football to enter the Second Division of the old Football Alliance. Walsall, as have many other clubs since, did not find League football so easy, and following two unsuccessful seasons dropped out, and did not again appear in first-class football until 1921, when the Northern Section of the Third Division was founded. Since then Walsall have appeared without break in this section, or the League South.

Their most note-worthy performance was when they defeated Arsenal in the F.A. Cup. Of that great Cup-fighting side only one player will be on duty at Stamford Bridge this afternoon. He is Gilbert Alsop, the dashing centre-forward, who, although not so young as he used to be, has developed into a first-class outside-left. Bournemouth will find, I feel sure, that Alsop, although a little slower than before the war, is as difficult as ever to dispossess.

Mr. Harry Hibbs, the former England and Birmingham goalkeeper, now manager of Walsall, has built up a good side in which youth and experience are carefully blended. Although Walsall have won their way to the Final by team-work, I am sure Mr. Hibbs will not mind me introducing one or two of his stars. Johnny Hancocks, for instance, the pint-sized right-winger, whom many good judges considered gave the best left-wing display of the season when he appeared for the Army against the R.A.F. at Stamford Bridge. Hancocks, a Wolverhampton boy who joined Walsall as an amateur eight years ago, has been admired

This Walsall side became the first ever to reach a national cup final, meeting Bournemouth in the final of the Division Three (South) Northern Section Cup at Stamford Bridge. Thousands of Walsall fans were amongst the 18,715 who saw a closely fought game end 1-0 to Bournemouth, with Walsall having cruel luck when Gilbert Alsop (hero of that 1933 win over Arsenal) twice went perilously close.

## SOUTHEND UNITED v WALSALL
### Kick-Off 3.30 p.m.

**SOUTHEND UNITED**
Blue Shirts (White Collars and Cuffs) White Knickers.

RIGHT WING      LEFT WING

Hankey
1

Jackson      Bell
2      3

Harris     Sheard     Walton F.
4     5     6

Smirke    Hamilton    Dudley    Thompson    Lane
7    8    9    10    11

*Referee :*      Linesmen :
Mr. H. Pearce     Mr. A. H. Blythe Blue Flag
      Mr. S. J. Isom Red Flag

Davies   Wilshaw   Darby   Talbot   Mullard
11   10   9   8   7

Newman    Foulkes    Crutchley
6    5    4

Shelton    Methley
3    2

Lewis
1

LEFT WING      RIGHT WING

**WALSALL**

### NEXT HOME MATCH

**FOOTBALL COMBINATION**
v

THURSDAY SEPT. 5th   **ARSENAL** RES.   KICK-OFF 6.15 p.m.

### HALF-TIME SCORES

| | | | | | | | |
|---|---|---|---|---|---|---|---|
| A | CHELSEA BOLTON WAN. | E | BURY FULHAM | J | ALDERSHOT BRISTOL CITY | N | MANSFIELD CRYSTAL PAL |
| B | EVERTON BRENTFORD | F | MILLWALL NEWCASTLE | K | BRIGHTON PORT VALE | O | NORTHAMPTON SWINDON T. |
| C | STOKE CITY CHARLTON | G | PLYMOUTH WEST HAM | L | BRISTOL ROV. READING | P | NORWICH C. CARDIFF CITY |
| D | WOLVES. ARSENAL | H | TOTTENHAM BIRMINGHAM | M | CLAPTON O' IPSWICH T. | R | QUEEN'S P. R WATFORD |

### THIRD DIVISION

1946.          For Agst.
Aug. 31—WALSALL ............... H
Sept. 4—Clapton Orient ............ A
   „ 7—Reading ................. A
   „ 12—IPSWICH O. (6.15) ... H
   „ 14—CRYSTAL PALACE   H
   „ 19—CLAPTON O. (6.0) ... H
   „ 21—Torquay United ......... A
   „ 28—MANSFIELD TOWN H
Oct. 5—Bristol Rovers .......... A
   „ 12—SWINDON TOWN ... H
   „ 19—Bournemouth & B. ... A
   „ 26—CARDIFF CITY ........ H
Nov. 2—Norwich City .......... A
   „ 9—NOTTS COUNTY ... H
   „ 16—Northampton T. ........ A
   „ 23—ALDERSHOT ........ H
   „ 30—F.A. Cup 1st Round
Dec. 7—EXETER CITY ........ H
   „ 14—(2) Port Vale ........... H
   „ 21—BRISTOL CITY ...... H
   „ 25—Watford ............... A
   „ 26—WATFORD ........... H
   „ 28—Walsall ................ A
1947.
Jan. 4—READING ............... H
   „ 11—(3) Brighton & H. ... A
   „ 18—Crystal Palace ......... A
   „ 25—(4) TORQUAY UTD. H
Feb. 1—Mansfield Town ...... A
   „ 8—(5) BRISTOL R. ...... H
   „ 15—Swindon Town ...... A
   „ 22—BOURNEMOUTH ... H
Mar. 1—(6) Cardiff City ...... A
   „ 8—NORWICH CITY ... H
   „ 15—Notts County .......... A
   „ 22—NORTHAMPTON T. H
   „ 29—Aldershot ............. A
April 4—Queen's Park Rang. H
   „ 5—BRIGHTON & H. ... H
   „ 7—QUEEN'S PARK R. ... H
   „ 12—Exeter City .......... A
   „ 19—PORT VALE .......... H
   „ 26—Bristol City .......... A
May 3—Ipswich Town .......... A

**LEAGUE TABLE**

### FOOTBALL COMBINATION LEAGUE MATCHES.

1946.          For Agt
Aug. 31—Reading ................. A
Sept. 5—ARSENAL (Thur) 6.15 H
   „ 7—IPSWICH TOWN ... H
   „ 14—Charlton Athletic ...... A
   „ 21—CARDIFF CITY ....... H
   „ 25 Plymouth Argyle (Wed) A
Oct. 3—CHARLTON (Thur)5.30 H
   „ 5—TOTTENHAM H. ... H
   „ 12—Swindon Town ........ A
   „ 16—Luton (Wed) `......... A
   „ 19—MILLWALL ............ H
   „ 23 Birmingham (Wed) .... A
   „ 26 Northampton Town .... A
Nov. 2—LUTON TOWN ........ H
   „ 9—Arsenal ................. A
   „ 16—PLYMOUTH A. ....... H
   „ 18—Tottenham Hotspur ... A
   „ 23—Cardiff City .......... A
   „ 30—NORTHAMPTON T. H
Dec. 7—Millwall ............... A
   „ 14—NORWICH CITY ... H
   „ 25—CLAPTON ORIENT H
   „ 26—Clapton Orient ....... A
   „ 28—READING ............. A
1947.
Jan. 4—Crystal Palace ......... A
   „ 11—SWINDON TOWN ... H
Apl. 12—BIRMINGHAM ...... H
   „ 19—Norwich City ......... A
   „ 26—Ipswich Town ......... A
May 1—CRYSTAL PALACE H

### FOOTBALL COMBINATION CUP COMPETITION.

1947.
Jan. 18—PORTSMOUTH ...... H
   „ 25—Portsmouth ........... A
Feb. 1—BRENTFORD ......... H
   „ 8—Reading ............... A
   „ 15—READING ............ H
   „ 22—Tottenham ............ A
Mar. 1—QUEENS PARK R. ... H
   „ 8—Brentford ............. A
   „ 15—ARSENAL ............ H
   „ 22—Arsenal ............... A
   „ 29—Southampton ......... A
Apl. 4—TOTTENHAM H. ... H
   „ 7—Queens Park Rangers ... A
May 3—SOUTHAMPTON ... H

**LEAGUE TABLE**

---

Walsall were nevertheless in good heart for the start of 1946/7 when normal divisional football returned. They travelled to Southend for the opening game of the new season, but were beaten 3-1. This game had originally been played in 1939 but was deleted from the record when war broke out. Interestingly enough, Walsall had also lost the original game 3-2, but the gate of 11,500 in 1946 was almost twice that of 1939.

One of the many sad aspects of the Second World War was that players who were full of promise in 1939 had passed their peak by 1946. One of these was inside forward Wally Brown, who had followed future international Johnny Hancocks from Oakengates in 1939 but was not quite the same player seven years later. After getting 4 goals in 22 games he moved into non-League football with Worcester City.

# Northampton Town Football Club Limited.

# Northampton Town v. WALSALL

## TUESDAY, APRIL 8th, 1947, kick-off 3 p.m.

### NORTHAMPTON TOWN

**McKEE**

2
**SMALLEY**

3
**ALLEN**

4
~~SMITH~~ *THOMPSON*

5
~~DENNISON~~ *STRATHIE*

6
~~THOMPSON~~ *BLUNT*

7
~~BRISCOE~~ *MORRALL*

8
~~JENKINS~~ *SMITH*

9
**GARRATT**

10
**HEASELGREAVE**

11
**ROBERTS**

Referee : H. PEARCE

Linesmen : H. N. COOK
W. A. BROOKS

*MULLARD*

**WILSHAW**
11

**LISHMAN**
10

~~DARBY~~
9

**WALSH**
8

*CAMPBELL* ~~MAUND~~
7

**NEWMAN**
6

**FOULKES**
5

**CRUTCHLEY**
4

**SKIDMORE**
3

**METHLEY**
2

**LEWIS**

## WALSALL

---

### RE-ARRANGED FIXTURES :

**No 1950**

Saturday, May 10th—WATFORD          ...          Away
Saturday, May 17th—CRYSTAL PALACE          Home
Saturday, May 31st—IPSWICH          ...          Home
ALDERSHOT (Home) to be arranged.

---

**Programme: Twopence**

The first post-war season certainly had its moments, however. On Easter Tuesday 8 April, Walsall were playing their fourth game in five days but they pulled off one of the biggest away wins not only in their own but in the whole of Football League history. They won 8-0 at Northampton with future England man Dennis Wilshaw and Albert Mullard both getting hat-tricks. Another fascinating aspect of that 8-0 win at Northampton was that it was on the same ground (in fact on their first-ever visit there) that they had lost 10-0 in November 1927. Harry Wait had been the goalkeeper in that 10-0 hammering and was Walsall's trainer at the time of the 8-0 triumph.

50

When Bert Williams moved to Wolves in September 1945, having already played for England in a wartime international, it seemed that he would be irreplaceable. Amazingly, Jackie Lewis, a diminutive goalkeeper from Boldmire St Michaels, immediately made the position his own. Following the resumption of League football in August 1946, he missed only 4 matches in five years. Although he was already twenty-six when he came into League football, he went on to play in a total of 286 games (including a spell at Hereford United). After retiring from the game, he kept a popular public house in his native Tamworth.

At the end of the war, several young players moved from First Division Wolves to Walsall – most of them with considerable success. One such player was Barnsley-born Irvine Methley, Originally a midfielder, he moved to the right flank of the defence on his arrival at Walsall in January 1946 and played in 92 consecutive games before an injury sustained against Notts County laid him low. Although he played for three more seasons, he was never quite the same. After his retirement in 1951, he ran a fish-and-chip business in the Walsall area for many years.

If the team of 1945/46 was one of the best ever to represent Walsall, that of 1947/48 came into the same category. Promotion was missed by just ten points; if this team which started the season had been maintained in its entirety for the whole campaign, then Walsall might just have pipped QPR and Bournemouth, the two teams that finished above them. From left to right, back row: G. Alsop, J. Robinson, H. Walters, H. Wait (trainer), R. Foulkes, W. Skidmore, I. Methley. Middle row: W. Guest, W. Brown, J. Lewis, D. Massart, K. Dellicott, A. Newman, D. Wilshaw. Front row: A. Mullard, J. Maund, W. Walsh, H. Hibbs (manager), K. Davies, J. Campbell, D. Lishman.

A key figure in the blistering start to the season was former Birmingham striker Dave Massart, who got a hat-trick in each of the first three home games. Though he played only 29 games for Walsall, he scored 23 goals and older fans still talk of his tremendous goalscoring feats. He moved on in March 1946 to Bury, who over the years have been a thorn in Walsall's flesh time and time again.

One of Walsall's best-ever signings was that of Johnny Devlin, a Scottish midfielder who was signed in December 1947 in a bid to boost Walsall's promotion bid. Promotion was not achieved, but skilful ball player, sharpshooter and penalty king Johnny, who was already thirty years old when he was signed from Kilmarnock, scored 50 goals in 166 games before moving to local club Bloxwich Strollers in 1952.

One of the young players that Johnny Devlin helped to develop during his five years with Walsall was young striker Phil Chapman. Phil had scarcely established himself in the reserves when he was thrown into the first team in September 1948. He scored in a 2-0 win and by the end of the season had banged home 28 goals. Alas, he never recaptured that sort of form and faded out of League football two years later, though he joined the Walsall police force and for many years was prolific for them.

White Shirts, Black Knickers.

## FULHAM

R　　　　　　　　FLACK　　　　　　　　L

2　　　　　　　3
FREEMAN　　　　BACUZZI

4　　　　　5　　　　　6
QUESTED　　　TAYLOR　　　BEASLEY

8　　　　　10
THOMAS, R.　　　JEZZARD

7　　　　　9　　　　　11
STEVENS　　　ROWLEY　　　McDONALD

Referee—　　　GILLETTE BLADE　　　Linesmen—
Mr. E. PLINSTON　　　　　　　Mr. W. THOMAS (Red Flag)
(Warrington)　　　　　　　　Mr. B. CARNE (Blue Flag)

11　　　　　9　　　　　7
CONDIE　　　CHAPMAN　　　ALDRED

10　　　　　8
DEVLIN　　　MULLARD

6　　　　　5　　　　　4
NEWMAN　　　FOULKES　　　CRUTCHLEY

3　　　　　2
WALTERS　　　JONES

LEWIS

L　　## WALSALL　　R

Claret & Blue Hooped Shirts, Black Knickers

**Patrons will be advised of any change in the above teams.**

Despite Phil Chapman's goals, Walsall's League position declined from third in 1947/48 to fourteenth in 1948/49, but their cup fighting tradition was maintained when they won 1-0 at Fulham's Craven Cottage in an FA Cup third round game in the same season that the Cottagers climbed into Division One

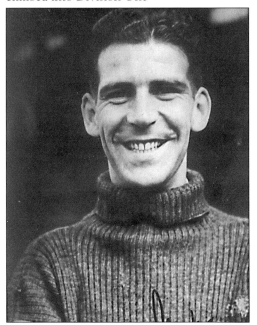

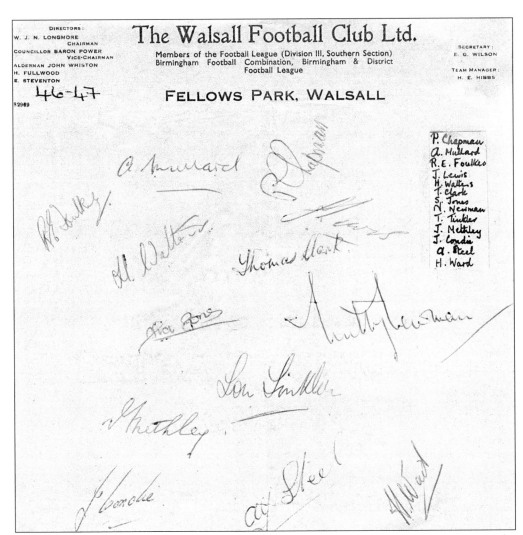

**DIRECTORS:**
W. J. N. LONGMORE
 CHAIRMAN
COUNCILLOR BARON POWER
 VICE-CHAIRMAN
ALDERMAN JOHN WHISTON
H. FULLWOOD
E. STEVENTON

**SECRETARY:**
E. G. WILSON

**TEAM MANAGER:**
H. E. HIBBS

# The Walsall Football Club Ltd.

Members of the Football League (Division III, Southern Section)
Birmingham Football Combination, Birmingham & District
Football League

46-47

82989

## FELLOWS PARK, WALSALL

P. Chapman
A. Mullard
R. E. Foulkes
J. Lewis
H. Walters
T. Clark
S. Jones
N. Newman
T. Tinkler
J. Methley
J. Condie
A. Steel
H. Ward

This autograph sheet was written on headed note paper with printing in claret in what was the last season in which Walsall played in their claret and blue hooped shirts. Though labelled 1946/47, it actually dates from the 1948/49 season.

*Below opposite:* Two of the members of the Fulham team that were the victims of Walsall's giant-killing act in 1949 were goalkeeper Doug Flack (left) and right flank defender Harry Freeman (right), both of whom moved to Walsall in the early 1950s near the end of their League careers.

55

This team group shows Walsall in their first season back in red and white shirts, the colour they had played in during their early days in the 1880s – although there was a striking contrast between the thick jerseys and long shorts of those early days and the more modern kit of the 1950s. From left to right, back row: G. Heseltine, R. Read, I. Methley, J. McLaughlin, W. Skidmore. Second row: H. Wait (trainer), H. Walters, A. Newman, J. Lewis, R. Foulkes, S. Jones, J. Maund (second team trainer). Front row: H. Hibbs (manager), G. Medd, J. Morris, J. Whitehouse, P. Chapman, J. Devlin, E. Betts, E. Wilson (secretary).

A catch question often tried on the unwary is 'Which Walsall defender of the early 1960s also played for England in the 1960s?' The answer is, of course, Jack Flavell, whose cricketing career blossomed after he had given up his active involvement in football. He took seven test wickets between 1962 and 1964 and in 1963 did the hat-trick for Worcestershire against Lancashire at Old Trafford.

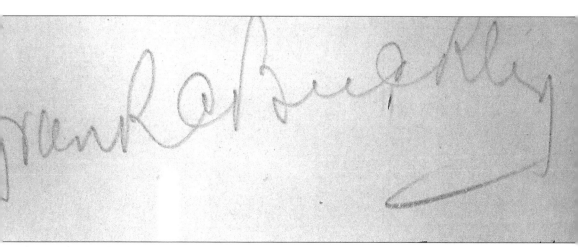

This much-prized autograph is of a legendary manager of yesteryear. Major Frank Buckley was capped as a player for England before the First World War and between the wars managed Norwich, Blackpool and Wolves. His ruthless discipline was legendary and after spells with Notts County and Leeds after the Second World War he took over at Walsall in 1953 at the age of seventy.

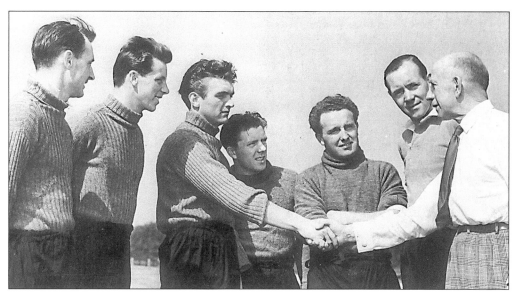

Hopes ran high when Major Buckley took over at Walsall, but despite trying out players galore he saw the club have to apply for re-election in three successive seasons before resigning in 1955. Here, we see him alongside assistant Jack Love welcoming five new players to the club in the summer of 1955. From left to right they are: Dave Walsh, Bill Gallier, Reg Davies, Sammy Moore and Hugh McLaren.

In the 1950s, much of the training was done on the actual pitch. This is a typical weekday scene at the old Fellows Park, with the stacks from Orgill's laundry prominent at the one end of the ground. The laundry survived until the mid-1960s.

Another scene from the 1950s, as the goal line is marked out at the laundry end with the traditional equipment of brush and bucket.

The wall at the laundry end of the ground always looked in danger when 'Fearless Fred' Morris raced down the right wing in the 1950s. A tremendous club servant and crowd-pleaser, he played a total of 230 games between 1950 and 1957 and later had a useful spell with Liverpool.

Jack Love did much to get Walsall back on an even keel when he joined them in March 1955, becoming one of the last of Major Buckley's many signings. He had been out of League football for nearly three years and was playing for Llanelli before his move to Walsall.

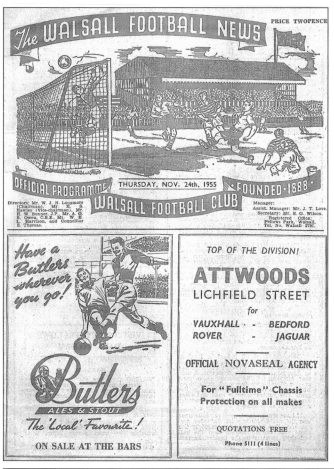

Jack Love was still active as a player when he took over from Major Buckley in 1955. Jack had been awarded the DFC while serving with the RAF during the Second World War and was a skilful midfielder. He did much to get Walsall back on the rails again after no fewer than four successive re-election applications. Jack Love was still acting as manager in a caretaker capacity when Walsall chalked up a heartening 6-1 win over Margate in an FA Cup first round replay in November 1955. One of the features of the Walsall scene in the 1950s, is that after little or no success for many years fans were still providing loyal support. A hardy band of 250 had travelled to Margate on the Saturday to see a 2-2 draw and, although the replay was played on a Thursday afternoon, 9,601 flocked into Fellows Park.

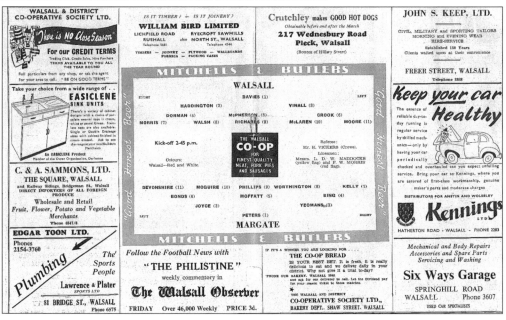

This League table might not look impressive from Walsall's point of view, but it was the beginning of a new era as for the first time in five seasons Walsall avoided the bottom two positions in Division Three (South) and so did not have to apply for re-election.

## DIVISION 3 SOUTH

|  | P | W | D | L | F | A | W | D | L | F | A | Pts |
|---|---|---|---|---|---|---|---|---|---|---|---|---|
| Leyton O | 46 | 18 | 3 | 2 | 76 | 20 | 11 | 5 | 7 | 30 | 29 | 66 |
| Brighton & H.A. | 46 | 20 | 2 | 1 | 73 | 16 | 9 | 5 | 9 | 39 | 34 | 65 |
| Ipswich T | 46 | 16 | 6 | 1 | 59 | 28 | 9 | 8 | 6 | 47 | 32 | 64 |
| Southend U | 46 | 16 | 4 | 3 | 58 | 25 | 5 | 7 | 11 | 30 | 55 | 53 |
| Torquay U | 46 | 11 | 10 | 2 | 48 | 21 | 9 | 2 | 12 | 38 | 42 | 52 |
| Brentford | 46 | 11 | 8 | 4 | 40 | 30 | 8 | 6 | 9 | 29 | 36 | 52 |
| Norwich C | 46 | 15 | 4 | 4 | 56 | 31 | 4 | 9 | 10 | 30 | 51 | 51 |
| Coventry C | 46 | 16 | 4 | 3 | 54 | 20 | 4 | 5 | 14 | 19 | 40 | 49 |
| Bournemouth | 46 | 13 | 6 | 4 | 39 | 14 | 6 | 4 | 13 | 24 | 37 | 48 |
| Gillingham | 46 | 12 | 3 | 8 | 38 | 28 | 7 | 7 | 9 | 31 | 43 | 48 |
| Northampton T | 46 | 14 | 3 | 6 | 44 | 27 | 6 | 4 | 13 | 23 | 44 | 47 |
| Colchester U | 46 | 14 | 4 | 5 | 56 | 37 | 4 | 7 | 12 | 20 | 44 | 47 |
| Shrewsbury T | 46 | 12 | 9 | 2 | 47 | 21 | 5 | 3 | 15 | 22 | 45 | 46 |
| Southampton | 46 | 13 | 6 | 4 | 60 | 30 | 5 | 2 | 16 | 31 | 51 | 44 |
| Aldershot | 46 | 9 | 9 | 5 | 36 | 33 | 3 | 7 | 13 | 34 | 57 | 40 |
| Exeter C | 46 | 10 | 6 | 7 | 39 | 30 | 5 | 4 | 14 | 19 | 47 | 40 |
| Reading | 46 | 10 | 2 | 11 | 40 | 37 | 5 | 7 | 11 | 30 | 42 | 39 |
| Q.P.R. | 46 | 10 | 7 | 6 | 44 | 32 | 4 | 4 | 15 | 20 | 54 | 39 |
| Newport Co | 46 | 12 | 2 | 9 | 32 | 26 | 3 | 7 | 13 | 26 | 53 | 39 |
| Walsall | 46 | 13 | 5 | 5 | 43 | 28 | 2 | 3 | 18 | 25 | 56 | 38 |
| Watford | 46 | 8 | 5 | 10 | 31 | 39 | 5 | 6 | 12 | 21 | 46 | 37 |
| Millwall | 46 | 13 | 4 | 6 | 56 | 31 | 2 | 2 | 19 | 27 | 69 | 36 |
| Crystal Palace | 46 | 7 | 3 | 13 | 27 | 32 | 5 | 7 | 11 | 27 | 51 | 34 |
| Swindon T | 46 | 4 | 10 | 9 | 18 | 22 | 4 | 4 | 15 | 16 | 56 | 30 |

During Walsall's time in the doldrums, several players joined who were to become an integral part of the club's promotion sides of the late 1950s and early '60s. One of these was Bill 'Chopper' Guttridge, who was signed by Major Buckley from one of the Major's former clubs, Wolves. A great crowd-pleaser, Bill stayed long enough to make over 200 appearances and is still talked of with affection by fans over forty years later.

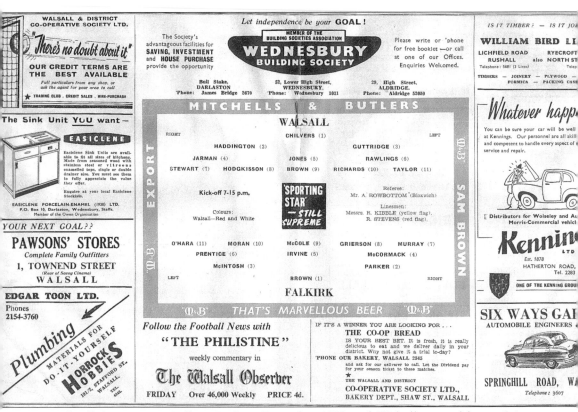

Floodlights came to Fellows Park in December 1957 and Walsall romped home 5-1 against Falkirk in the official opening game, with flame-haired Tommy Brownlee getting a hat-trick.

Tommy Brownlee was one of the many Scots to join Walsall in the 1940s and '50s. Although he never held down a regular place, his record of 14 goals in 30 games bears favourable comparison with that of most strikers. He moved to York in 1958 and later played for Workington, Netherfield and Bradford City (returning to League football after an absence of four seasons to score 15 goals in 26 games for the Bantams).

In the early days of floodlit football, teams from the lower divisions eagerly sought prestigious games against 'big' clubs. This letter, written by long-serving Walsall secretary Ernie Wilson, did not succeed in tempting Everton to play under the Walsall floodlights. Some interesting games took place in the late 1950s, however, Derby County and Leicester City being amongst the teams to come to Fellows Park.

**DIRECTORS:**
COUN. ERNEST THOMAS (CHAIRMAN)
H. S. HAWLEY (VICE CHAIRMAN)
W. J. N. LONGMORE
H. W. BONNER, J. P.
A.G.B. OWEN, C.B.E.
W. H. L. HARRISON

# The Walsall Football Club Ltd

## FELLOWS PARK · WALSALL

TEAM MANAGER: W. MOORE

**COLOURS**
RED SHIRTS WITH WHITE COLLARS AND CUFFS, WHITE SHORTS, RED STOCKINGS WITH WHITE TOPS.

SECRETARY
E. G. WILSON
TELEPHONE
WALSALL · 2791

3rd. September, 1958.

Mr. W. Dickinson,
Everton F.C. Ltd.,
Goodison Park,
LIVERPOOL.4.

Dear Mr. Dickinson,

    May we extend to your Club an invitation to play a Friendly Floodlight Match at Fellows Park during the current Season on a date to suit your convenience, and on F.A. Cup-tie terms. A visit from your Club would be an exceptional attraction and a very considerable attendance may be anticipated. The match would be looked upon not only as a financial benefit but as an object lesson in First Class Football to our Players and Supporters. Will you please give this matter your kind consideration in due course, incidentally the Floodlighting installation at this Ground is First Class and was completed last Season.

    Looking forward to hearing from you.

                        Yours faithfully,

                        (E.G. Wilson).
                        Secretary:

One of the participants in some of those early floodlight games was giant goalkeeper John Savage, who played only 51 games after moving from Manchester City in 1958 but is still talked of forty years later on account of his tremendous reach and massive clearances. He also became the first Walsall goalkeeper ever to be sent off.

April 1959 brought the last issue of the eight-page match programme which had served Walsall with very few changes since its inception in 1920 – a total of over 1,500 issues, since there were full-size editions for reserve games in those days.

The following August a pocket-sized issue was launched. This survived for eight seasons with few changes, but some fans argued that its thirty pages contained less material than the eight pages of the old format.

*Five*

# The Glory Years
# and Beyond

After the 1950s had seen Walsall surviving four successive re-election applications in Division Three (South), the new Fourth Division brought an immediate change in fortune. From left to right, back row: P. Billingham, A. McPherson, T. Rawlings, J. Christie, J. Davies, S. Jones, J. Sharples. Third row: V. Potts (trainer), A. Wright, R. Faulkner, C. Askey, K. Ball, A. Walker, K. Hill, J. Janman (coach). Second row: W. Moore (manager), A. Richards, W. Guttridge, K. Hodgkisson, E. Wilson (secretary). Front row: F. Gregg, C. Taylor.

After narrowly missing promotion in 1959, Walsall went up to Division Three in 1960 and to Division Two in 1961. This team was undoubtedly one of finest ever to represent Walsall. From left to right, back row: R. Faulkner, J. Davies, J. Christie, J. Sharples, K. Ball, J. Dudley, T. Rawlings. Second row: A. Richards, A. McPherson, W. Guttridge, H. Haddington, K. Hodgkisson, C. Taylor. Front row: K. Hill, N. Rowe, C. Askey, T. Foster.

Walsall were lucky enough to possess two of their greatest ever strikers at this period of their history. Tony Richards actually wrote in for a trial in 1954 and his tally of 195 goals in 354 games included 26 in the Fourth Division promotion season of 1959/60 and 36 in the Third Division promotion season of 1960/61.

Colin Taylor came from local West Midland League club Stourbridge in 1958 and his tally of 190 goals in 502 games in three spells with the club included 21 in the Fourth Division promotion season of 1959/60 and 33 in the Third Division promotion season of 1960/61.

Manager during that unforgettable double promotion run was 'Iron Man' Bill Moore. He had been Aston Villa's trainer when they won the FA Cup in 1957, took over at Fellows Park in December 1957 and stayed until 1963, later returning for a rather less successful spell from 1969 to 1972. His partnership with chairman Ernie Thomas in his first spell was one of the most successful manager-chairman relationships in the whole of Walsall's history.

For an all-too-brief spell Walsall seemed capable of taking the Second Division by storm. In one of the most memorable games ever played at Fellows Park, they won the opening game of the season 4-3 against Sunderland, for whom the one and only Brian Clough was making his debut.

Leading Walsall out in those glory days was Albert McPherson, who succeeded Harry Haddington as captain when the latter suffered a broken leg in 1960. Albert played a total of 367 first team games up to 1964 and later had a long spell on the West Brom coaching staff. Following Albert onto the field in this picture is Ken Hill, a Walsall born and bred midfielder who had two spells in the Saddlers' midfield either side of a short spell with Norwich. He still lives in Walsall and takes a keen interest in the club forty years after those great promotion days. One of the secrets of Walsall's success in gaining successive promotions was that they were able to field a virtually unchanged team week after week. In 1959/60, when they topped Division Four, ten players appeared in 35 games or more. The single major change that season came in December when Jimmy Dudley was signed from West Brom and replaced Peter Billingham. Despite the League success that season, however, Walsall were knocked out of the FA Cup by Midland League Peterborough at Fellows Park. In 1960/61, they finished as runners-up in Division Three. Eight players appeared in 35 games or more and there was still a good deal of consistency in the positions that were subject to change: Granville Palin played 27 games on the right flank of defence, Ray Faulkner played 21 games as an attacking midfielder and Tommy Wilson played 28 games up front. Despite being unbeaten at home in League games, Walsall again went out of the FA Cup to non-League opposition: this time it was Yeovil of the Southern League that caused their blushes.

A record gate of 25,453 saw Walsall beat the mighty Newcastle in their second home game on 29 August 1961. Hero of that win over Newcastle was Bill Younger, who netted a remarkable twenty-five yard shot into the laundry goal. Bill played only 8 first team gates for Walsall, but scored 5 goals before moving on to Doncaster Rovers.

One of the saddest nights in Walsall's history was 24 May 1963, when a serious injury to goalkeeper Alan Boswell (in the days before substitutes were allowed) meant that they had to play most of the vital final game with Charlton with ten men. A crowd of 16,761 saw them go down 2-1 when a draw would have kept them up. Here we see 'Bozzer' helped off the field by trainers Vic Potts and Alf Wood after suffering a cracked cheekbone. There was a particular irony in Charlton winning at Walsall in 1963 and so avoiding relegation, as just over thirty years earlier their manager Frank Hill had been in the Arsenal side beaten by Walsall in the famous FA Cup giant-killing. It was unfortunate for Walsall in that this was a replayed match, the original encounter taking place on 20 May 1963 and being abandoned at half-time following a massive thunderstorm. The score in the aborted game was 0-0, with Walsall well on top. Arguably, with Boswell reaching the half-way point unscathed, Walsall would have picked up the point they needed and avoided relegation. Furthermore, in the replayed game, striker Graham Newton was also injured in the first half and Walsall played for the majority of the match with only nine fit players. Agonisingly enough, the possibility of staying up had been achieved with magnificent wins at Chelsea and Newcastle in the preceding matches. Although Boswell recovered by the beginning of the following season, he did not play for Walsall again. A squabble with chairman Ernie Thomas led to moving to Shrewsbury, for whom he played 256 games, before later having short spells with Wolves, Bolton and Port Vale.

After promotion in successive seasons and then relegation two seasons later, Walsall settled down to an unbroken spell of sixteen seasons in Division Three. Here Alf Wood, the former Coventry goalkeeper who moved up from coach to manager in October 1964, greets Mick Evans, Trevor Meath and Trevor West soon after his appointment.

One of the young players whom Alf Wood particularly encouraged was Allan Clarke, who scored 46 goals in 82 games before moving on to Fulham in March 1966. Later of course, Allan moved on to Leicester and Leeds and won 19 full England caps.

Another member of the Walsall staff in the mid-1960s who went on to become a household name was Arthur Cox. He was the youngest-ever club coach when he joined Walsall in 1965 at the age of twenty-five after his own playing career had been shattered by injury. He moved to Aston Villa in 1968 as assistant manager, has since managed Chesterfield, Derby and Newcastle and in recent times was part of the England set-up under Kevin Keegan.

During Bill Harrison's time as chairman from 1964 until his death in 1968, Walsall tried many new ventures, including flying to an away match at Southend in February 1966. In this picture Allan Clarke is having his papers checked, with trainer Arthur Cox and vice-chairman Ron Harrison in the queue behind him.

Walsall did not win anything at first team level in the mid-1960s, but their reserve team won the Second Division of the Football Combination in 1966/67. From left to right, back row: Harry Middleton, Trevor Meath, Bob Wesson, Roy Cross, Gerry Harris, Colin Harrison. Front row: Paul Coton, Jimmy McEwan, Gerry Summers, Geoff Morris, Roger Smith.

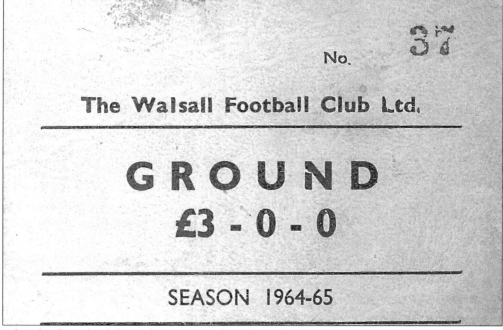

After the flourish of the early 1960s, results did not always go Walsall's way for the rest of the decade – but they usually gave value for money. This 1964/65 season ticket cost just £3 (around 13p per game with reserve games for free).

There were quite a number of false dawns in the later 1960s. In 1966/67, Walsall kicked off with three potentially prolific strikers: the youthful Roger Jones and vastly experienced Derek Pace and George Kirby. Sadly, Roger did not break through into the first team, Derek scored only one goal and George, after scoring 11 goals, was released at the end of the season.

The 1968/69 season began full of hope after a promotion bid had fizzled out in the previous campaign. This line-up contained plenty of experience. From left to right, back row: Alan Baker, John Harris, Stan Jones, Alf Biggs, Trevor Meath, Jimmy Murray, John Burckitt. Middle row: Roy Cross, Mick Evans, Bob Wesson, Phil Parkes, Keith Ball, Stan Bennett, Jimmy McEwan (trainer). Front row: Geoff Morris, Nick Atthey, Tommy Watson, Ron Lewin (manager), Mike Tindall, Colin Harrison, Frank Gregg.

The season could still have gone either way as midfielder Jimmy McMorran and manager Ron Lewin set out to catch the coach for an away game just before the FA Cup third round tie against Tottenham. Sadly, the game was called off and the game against Spurs was lost 1-0 after a brave struggle. Soon afterwards, Ron Lewin was sacked.

Bill Moore returned as manager early in 1969 but he suffered many disappointments, including the calling off of this game at Fellows Park after a local referee had found the pitch unplayable.

John Smith had enjoyed some success as a
player at West Ham, Tottenham and
Swindon, but as Walsall manager from
October 1972 to March 1973 things did not
go his way.

John had earlier served Walsall both as player and coach and is putting Johnny Woodward,
Nick Atthey, Jimmy Dainty and Alan Deakin through their paces at the Hillary Street end of
Fellows Park in this 1971 picture.

Over the years several Walsall football teams have tried their hand at cricket. Here we see Stan Jones, Jimmy McEwan, Alan Deakin, Mick Evans, Stan Bennett and Colin Harrison taking the field in the summer of 1971.

Just as Tony Richards had done nearly twenty years earlier, Bernie Wright wrote in for a trial at Walsall in 1971 after being released by Birmingham City. The swashbuckling striker had two spells with Walsall (with a short stint for Everton sandwiched inbetween), netting 48 goals in 196 games but just as importantly putting himself about to create opportunities for players such as Alan Buckley and George Andrews to cash in on.

This is how Fellows Park looked from the air in its latter days after the laundry building had been removed in 1965.

For many years Walsall had dreamed of a spectacular new stadium. Here is one of those dreams being surveyed by Ron Harrison (chairman from 1968 to 1972), secretary Ernie Wilson and an architect. Sadly, that vision of the future did not come to fruition.

Something that did happen in 1972/73, however, was that Walsall used no fewer than seven different goalkeepers in the season, among them John Osborne, who played just three games on loan from West Brom (for whom he played over 300 games and won an FA Cup winners medal in 1968).

Ian Turner was another player who kept goal for Walsall in 1972/73, while on loan from Grimsby. He returned on a more permanent basis in the late 1970s and played a further 43 games.

By the time Walsall were making national news in January 1975 by putting both Manchester United and Newcastle United out of the FA Cup, Mick Kearns had arrived from Oxford to make the goalkeeping position his own. Here he receives one of the many Man of the Match awards that came his way in the course of 322 games in two spells between 1973 and 1984. The presenter is local businessman John Dore.

Players, manager and physiotherapist relax in the dressing room following the remarkable 3-2 win after extra time over Manchester United in the third round FA Cup replay on 7 January 1975. From left to right, back row: George Andrews, Brian Taylor, Bernie Wright, Doug Fraser (manager), Alan Buckley, Alan Birch. Front row: Bob Davies (physiotherapist), John Saunders.

Alan Buckley in a typical celebratory pose after scoring. In two spells as player he netted 205 goals in 483 games between 1973 and 1985 and two of the goals came in that Manchester United win. He was of course also manager intermittently between 1979 and 1986.

George Andrews (here seen without his beard for once) headed the only goal of the FA Cup fourth round tie against Newcastle on 24 January 1975, which was contested on a pitch scarcely fit for play.

Giant-killing was again the order of the day on 28 January 1978 when Alun Evans got a last minute match-winner against Leicester in a FA Cup fourth round tie. Here, Alan celebrates in the dressing room with Colin Harrison and Dave Serella to the left and Mick Bates, Brian Caswell and Alan Birch to the right.

Walsall finally lost their Third Division place in 1979 but bounced straight back up again in 1979/80 with this side. From left to right, back row: Jimmy Williams, Ian Paul, John Horne, Ian Turner, Ron Green, Roy McDonough, Ricky Sbragia, Colin Harrison. Front row: Tony Macken, Alan Buckley, Dave Serella, Don Penn, Steve Waddington, Brian Caswell, Jimmy Kelly.

A Walsall servant both man and boy, Ray Train had spells as a player at the beginning of his career in the late 1960s and at the end of his career in the late 1980s. He also had a spell as caretaker manager early in 1990.

Another great servant of Walsall Football Club was chairman Ken Wheldon, who stepped in to save the club from bankruptcy in 1972 and stayed at the helm until 1985. A man of mystery – it was rumoured that he had been on Mansfield's books under another name as a player – he was a shrewd financier, although he shipped rough water when possible ground-sharing schemes with first Wolves and then Birmingham were announced. He died in the mid-1990s and one will never forget some of his inimitable quips, such as that he had arrived at the club in 1972 to find it 'wrapped in waste paper and tied up with string'.

Ken Wheldon was a man of few words, as this brief report to shareholders in 1980 indicates.

# Report of the Directors

**The Directors present their Report and the audited accounts of the Company for the year ended 30th June, 1980.**

---

**ACTIVITIES :**

The principal activities of the Company continue to be those of a Professional Football League Club.

**STATE OF AFFAIRS :**

The financial results for the year are shown in the annexed accounts.

The Directors consider that the Company's state of affairs is satisfactory and they do not recommend the payment of a dividend in respect of the year under review.

**FIXED ASSETS :**

The attached accouts and schedules show details of changes in fixed assets during the year.

**FREEHOLD LAND & BUILDINGS :**

The current market value of the Company's freehold land and buildings is considered by the Directors to be considerably in excess of the book value.

**DIRECTORS :**

The undermentioned persons served as Directors of the Company throughout the year and their respective shareholdings in the Company were as follows :—

|  | 30.6.80 | 30.6.79 |
|---|---|---|
| K. E. Wheldon ... ... ... | 8,000 | 8,000 |
| J. A. Harris ... ... ... | 6,476 | 6,476 |
| R. Homden ... ... ... | 6,575 | 6,575 |
| S. E. Boler ... ... ... | 7,000 | 7,000 |
| B. E. Bradnack ... ... ... | 6,739 | 6,488 |

The Directors retiring by rotation are Messrs. R. Homden and S. E. Boler and, being eligible, offer themselves for re-election.

**AUDITORS :**

A resolution for the re-appointment of the Auditors, Messrs. Pembridge and Company, will be proposed at the forthcoming Annual General Meeting.

By Order of the Board,

H. J. WESTMANCOAT,

13th March, 1981.

*Secretary.*

One of several meetings held in 1982 to protest at the idea of sharing a ground with Wolves. Addressing the gathering is Barry Blower, who later became club chairman and, at the beginning of the new millennium, was club president.

Ground-sharing was forgotten by the time Walsall won the nation's hearts again by reaching the Milk Cup semi-final in 1984, beating Arsenal at Highbury en route. Amazingly, in the first leg of the semi-final at Anfield they twice equalized to draw 2-2 with the mighty Liverpool. Here we see Phil Neal turning a Richard O'Kelly cross into his own net.

Kevin Summerfield executes the neatest of chips to beat Bruce Grobbelaar for the second equalizer.

Three stalwarts from Walsall FC Supporters Club, Ken Morrell, John Wilson and Bernard Johnston, celebrate the remarkable Milk Cup run with the presentation of a clock.

A season later Walsall were giant-killers again. This 1985 picture at Coventry's Highfield Road tells its own story.

Walsall players applaud their fans after that great win at Coventry.

The management team in those Milk Cup glory days of 1984 and 1985, assistant Garry Pendrey and manager Alan Buckley.

Alan Buckley is here pictured with stalwart defender Steve Baines, who later became a Football League referee and has several times taken charge of Walsall games.

Exciting little winger Ian Handysides starred in several superb Walsall wins in the mid-1980s, including that 3-0 Milk Cup win at Coventry in 1985. Sadly he developed a brain tumour and died in 1990 at the age of twenty-seven.

Starfinder supreme Ron Jukes had two separate spells as Walsall's chief scout. In his first stint, the nucleus of the 1960 and 1961 promotion teams were his discoveries. In his second term, half of the team that held Liverpool in the Milk Cup semi-final were brought to Walsall as juniors by Ron. He later served Wolves, Birmingham, Derby and Shrewsbury and at the beginning of the twenty-first century was at Hereford.

Ron Jukes is pictured here on the occasion of his seventieth birthday in May 1998, with just a few of his discoveries of earlier years. From left to right, back row: Brian Caswell, Stan Jones, Allan Clarke, Mick Kearns. Front row: Frank Gregg, Ron Jukes, Nick Atthey, Colin Harrison, Mark Rees. All except Mick Kearns were signed by Ron as youngsters.

## Six
# Promotion Again and the New Millennium

However attractively Walsall played in the mid-1980s and however many giant-killing acts they pulled off, they didn't manage to climb out of Division Three. Finance again became a problem after Ken Wheldon had moved on to Birmingham in 1986. Barry Blower, leader of the action group, somehow found a rich new chairman, who flew in by helicopter in 1987.

A new management team was immediately appointed by new chairman Terry Ramsden. It consisted of former Arsenal winger Tommy Coakley and former Bristol City defender Gerry Sweeney.

Another key figure of the new regime was Tom Bradley, who moved from Willenhall Town as physiotherapist and stayed until his retirement fifteen years later.

Tommy Coakley was very much a players' man. Here he applauds his team off the field.

Peter Hart watches the mascots shaking hands in front of referee Ray Lewis before a game against Darlington.

Peter Hart was one of the players who survived from the struggling side of the early 1980s via the Milk Cup giant-killing teams of the mid-'80s. After moving from Huddersfield in 1980, he played 479 games, mainly in defence, and skippered the 1988 promotion team. Peter was later ordained into the Anglican Church.

Every team needs a good, reliable goalkeeper if they are to win anything and Fred Barber, signed from Everton in 1986, played in every game in 1987/88 as Walsall went up to Division Two, after a season in which they played a total of 62 League and cup games.

Rarely has money been better spent than the £30,000 that took Trevor Christie from Notts County to Walsall in 1986. He got 11 goals in the promotion season and was a handful for any defence.

Here Trevor celebrates a typical goal at the laundry end at Fellows Park.

Not only was there purposeful soccer on the field during the Ramsden-Coakley regime of the late 1980s, but every effort was made to generate an atmosphere off it. Fellows Park in its lattermost days echoed again to the sound of a band before games.

There was also the glamour of cheerleaders in the club's colours.

Nor must we forget the fans. Octogenarian Kitty Lyons (here being greeted by Barry Blower) had watched Walsall in the 1920s and saw them win promotion to Division Two in 1988.

These are the men who did it – the promotion team of 1988. From left to right, back row: Ken Oliver (coach), Bobby Hutchinson, Andy Dornan, Peter Hart, Willie Naughton, Fred Barber, Kenny Mower, Mark Jones, Graeme Forbes, Trevor Christie, Paul Jones, Dr McKechnie. Front row: David Kelly, Craig Shakespeare, Nicky Cross, Mark Goodwin, Gerry Sweeney (assistant manager), Tommy Coakley (manager), Phil Hawker, Mark Rees, Mark Taylor, Ray Train. Fortunate indeed are those fans who saw the powerful Walsall side just after the war, the promotion sides of 1959/60 and 1960/61 and the promotion side of 1988. All these teams were great credits to their respective managers: Harry Hibbs, Bill Moore and Tommy Coakley. The trio came from vastly different backgrounds – Harry had been a Birmingham and England goalkeeper, Bill a no-nonsense defender with Mansfield and Stoke, while Tommy enjoyed a brief spell as Arsenal's right-winger and had managed Bishop Stortford. None of the three had managed a Football League club before, but all fostered an unquenchable team spirit, underpinned with strength at the back and in midfield and opportunism up front. All three Walsall managers lost vital players and declined from the pinnacle of their respective successes: Dave Massart moved to Bury in 1947, Tommy Wilson suffered injury in 1961 and David Kelly moved to West Ham in 1988.

Mark Rees, seen here scoring against Rotherham in that 1984 Milk Cup run, frightened many defenders with his blistering pace. Although he played only a few games in the 1987/88 promotion run, he went on to have a useful spell as an attacking right flank defender.

Even when Walsall were enjoying some glorious times in the 1980s, fans often looked back to the heroes of the '60s, many of whom were still playing in charity games. Here is a typical Saddlers All Stars line-up. From left to right, back row: John Sharples, Bill Guttridge, Keith Ball, Granville Palin, Gordon Wills, Ray Wiggin, Graham Newton. Front row: Tony Richards, Colin Taylor, Albert McPherson, George Meek, Ken Hodgkisson.

Spring Bank Holiday 30 May 1988 was the day that promotion to Division Two was clinched with a David Kelly hat-trick in a play off final replay against Bristol City at Bescot. Here, David climbs into the stand after the game, clutching the ball with which he had scored his goals.

Relationships between the club itself and the Supporters Club have fluctuated over the years, but in that 1988 promotion year all was sweetness and light as the supporters club presented the football club with a mini-bus. Here, manager Tommy Coakley, players Fred Barber, Andy Dornan, Craig Shakespeare, Willie Naughton and Trevor Christie give the thumbs up as long-serving supporters club official Ken Morrell (who also had a spell on the board) takes the wheel.

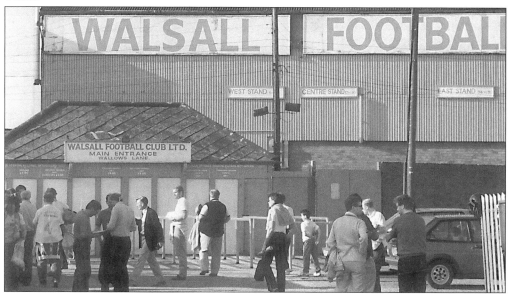

After the 1988 promotion glory things went badly wrong. A slump in the Japanese stock market had serious consequences for Terry Ramsden, who had to give up the Walsall FC chairmanship to try to sort out his own financial problems, and as the team suffered relegation in 1989 and 1990 gates inevitably declined. Just a trickle of a crowd is pictured here arriving for one of the last games at Fellows Park in the spring of 1990.

WALSALL

FELLOWS PARK OUR HOME SINCE 1903.
OUR LAST LEAGUE GAME AT FELLOWS PARK.
TONIGHT IS OUR 1,577th GAME ON THIS GROUND
AS A FOOTBALL LEAGUE CLUB.

AUTOGLASS

BARCLAYS LEAGUE
DIVISION THREE
Tuesday May 1st 1990
Kick Off 7.30 p.m.

# ROTHERHAM
# UNITED

with The History of
Fellows Park £1.00

The last League game at Fellows Park attracted just 5,697 fans and the 1-1 draw against Rotherham was far too late to keep the team in Division Three. A special fifty-two page match programme was produced, selling at just £1. It now fetches £10 to £20 in the second-hand market.

As Fellows Park closed the new Bescot Stadium opened with Sir Stanley Matthews there to perform the opening ceremony. Here the one and only Wizard of Dribble is photographed with Barry Blower, a fan of over forty years who had led the campaign to keep Walsall FC in Walsall in the early 1980s and who was now chairman. The sadness of many fans at leaving the familiar environment of Fellows Park was offset by the thought of moving into the more plush surroundings of the Bescot Stadium. Would the new ground be the scene of the sort of giant-killing acts seen at Fellows Park in the past, with the likes of Arsenal, Manchester United and Newcastle biting the dust? Pessimists pointed out that the Bescot had only half the capacity of Fellows Park and that there was a certain irony in the fact that, after relegation in two successive seasons, the team was kicking off in a new stadium with a Division Four match. Optimists, however, suggested that in these circumstances things could only get better. Alarmingly, the gate of 5,219 for the opening League game against Torquay compared unfavourably with that of 5,697 for the last League game, against Rotherham United, at Fellows Park. Furthermore, the omens were not good in the Torquay match as Walsall defender Matt Bryant (on loan from Bristol City) put the ball in his own net on his Football League debut. The game finished 2-2 and, although the ensuing season had its ups and downs, it finished on a high note when Walsall wrecked Blackpool's promotion hopes with a 2-0 win in front of a crowd of 8,051.

A crowd of 9,551 was present to see the first game at Bescot on 18 August 1990. Aston Villa provided the opposition and won this friendly encounter 4-0. Walsall's attacks all came to nothing, including this one as Villa 'keeper Nigel Spink beats Martin Goldsmith to the ball.

Ron Green was a member of Walsall's 1979/80 promotion team and, after spells with Scunthorpe, Wimbledon, Shrewsbury and Manchester City, was back at Walsall to play in the first 44 League games at the new Bescot Stadium in 1990/91.

Groundsman Roger Johnson carefully tended the Fellows Park pitch for over a decade. These two pictures show just how lovingly he got the new Bescot pitch into shape.

The new manager for the first season at the new Bescot Stadium was Kenny Hibbitt, who in his playing days had been one of the best uncapped midfielders of the 1970s and '80s in the course of well over 600 games for Bradford Park Avenue, Wolves, Coventry and Bristol Rovers. These were the players who did their best to kick start the 1990/91 season back in Division Four with a new ground but limited resources. In the circumstances they did reasonably well to finish as high as sixteenth (the club's lowest ever position in Division Four, which is now Division Three). From left to right, back row: Kenny Mower, Steve O'Hara, Fred Barber, Graeme Forbes, Ron Green, Dave Barnett, Dean Smith. Middle row: Ken Gutteridge (chief scout), Eric McManus (youth development officer), John Kelly, Chris Marsh, Martin Goldsmith, Chris Hutchings, Tony Grealish, Tom Bradley (physiotherapist). Front row: Darren Riley, Rod McDonald, Phil Witehouse, Stuart Rimmer, Kenny Hibbitt (manager), Peter Skipper, Billy Millen, Alex Taylor, Adrian Littlejohn. A total of twenty-eight players were used in that first season at the Bescot, as Kenny Hibbitt tried to build a team capable of winning promotion but with no money to spend on transfers. Defender Colin Methuen was signed from Carlisle in November, just one month short of his thirty-fifth birthday, and did not miss a single game for over a year. Indeed, defensively, Walsall did quite well with just 51 goals conceded in 46 games. On the other hand, only 48 goals were scored and it was a sad reflection on the club's dire financial straits that top-scorer Stuart Rimmer had to be sold in February to Barnsley (after scoring 18 of the club's total of 40 goals at that point). Another telling statistic is that of the many players tried during the campaign, nine played in fewer than 10 games.

Kenny Hibbert looks relaxed as he prepares
for the new campaign.

Mike Cecere (number 10) challenges for a high ball in the 2-2 draw against Aldershot in October
1990 in a rather empty looking Bescot stadium. In fact 3,567 were present and this was the last but
one visit of the Shots to Walsall before they dropped out of the Football League.

One of the brightest spots of Walsall's unhappy spell as the 1980s turned into the '90s was the goalscoring form of diminutive Stuart Rimmer. Though he spent only a little more than two years with Walsall, he played on two different home grounds and in three different divisions and his record of 44 goals in 106 games was quite remarkable, considering that he was playing in a struggling team for the whole of his time with the club. Here, he scores a typical opportunistic goal having made space between two opponents.

Another very popular player during the lean spell in the early 1990s was Charlie Ntamark. A Cameroon international, he made his Walsall debut in the first League game at Bescot in August 1990 and in the course of 336 games he played in defence, midfield and up front, played under two different managers and missed only seven games in the 1994/95 promotion season.

When goals were scarce Rod McDonald, a signing from now defunct Colne Dynamoes, battled away. Here he celebrates a goal with Charlie Ntamark.

McDonald celebrates another goal with long-serving Chris Marsh. Rod got 46 goals between 1990 and 1994, while Chris is still with the Saddlers in the year 2000 with well over 450 games behind him in all parts of the field.

Although the early 1990s did not bring Walsall much cup glory and in fact one embarrassing defeat (by Yeovil in 1991), they did successfully negotiate a potential banana skin with this Rod McDonald match-winner at Aylesbury in November 1990.

After a period of uncertainty behind the scenes, Jeff Bonser, who had been a director since 1988, became chairman in 1991. By 1992/93 the team reached the playoffs. The injection of experienced locally-born striker Wayne Clarke into the attack added spark to a useful side, although as this larger-than-usual team photograph implies it was not exactly a settled line-up and no fewer than twenty-five players were used during the campaign. From left to right, back row: Tom Bradley (physiotherapist), Scott Ollerenshaw, Kevin Macdonald, Colin Methven, Steph O'Hara, Mark Gayle, Jim Norris, Wayne Clarke, Dean Smith, Stuart Ryder, Charlie Ntamark, Eric McManus (youth development officer). Front row: Chris Marsh, Mike Cecere, Richard Brown, Chris Demetrios, David Edwards, Kenny Hibbitt (manager), Rod McDonald, Steve Winter, Richard Knight, Derek Statham, Wayne Williams.

Jeff Bonser sits happily at the wheel of the club minibus with three Supporters Club officials: Bernard Johnston, John Wilson and Ken Morrell.

One of the most popular signings of the early 1990s was Martyn O'Connor. This attacking midfielder had a spell on loan from Crystal Palace near the end of 1992/93 and signed more permanently a year later.

In the 1994/95 promotion season Martyn O'Connor netted a total of five penalties, including two in one game against Scarborough.

By this time Chris Nicholl had taken over as manager. Pictured here in his Aston Villa playing days with Ron Saunders, his no-nonsense approach bore a striking resemblance to that of his old boss. Both as player and manager, he had a fine record for achieving promotion for his clubs. When Walsall climbed out of Division Four in 1995 at the end of Chris's first season, they ended their longest-ever spell in the bottom division of the Football League. One fascinating aspect of Chris Nicholl's highly successful first season was that he did not win a Manager of the Month award until the last month of the season, which is when it counted.

One of the assets that Chris Nicholl discovered when he took over at Bescot in September 1994 was Kevin Wilson, who had arrived from Notts County two months earlier. He was already thirty-three years of age but didn't miss a game for two and a half seasons and his 16 goals were a major factor in securing promotion, not to mention the support he gave to Kyle Lightbourne, who ended the campaign with 23 goals.

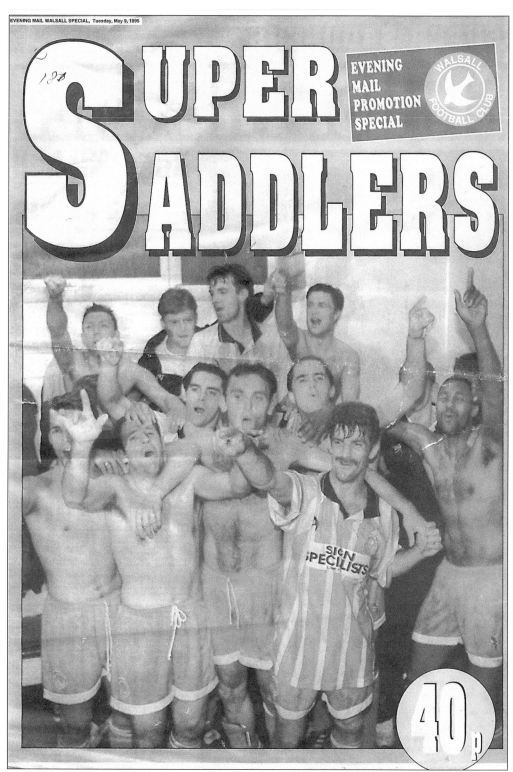

# SUPER SADDLERS

EVENING MAIL PROMOTION SPECIAL

WALSALL FOOTBALL CLUB

SIGN SPECIALISTS

40p

A promotion special from the *Evening Mail*.

After three seasons at the helm, in which he took Walsall from the middle of Division Three to the middle of Division Two, Chris Nicholl went into retirement. He was succeeded by Walsall's first continental manager, Jan Sorensen, who had won 15 Danish caps as a powerful midfielder. Sorensen brought plenty of attacking flair to the club and under his leadership Walsall reached the fourth round of both the Coca Cola Cup and the FA Cup and the semi-final of the Auto Windscreens Trophy.

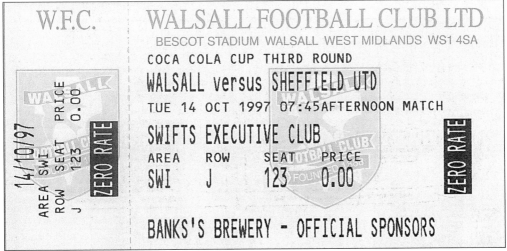

Thrilling games early in the season included Coca Cola Cup successes over both Nottingham Forest and Sheffield United. The above ticket is labelled as being for an 'afternoon match', although the kick-off is clearly 7.45.

A key figure in the exciting football played by Sorenson's Saddlers was Roger Boli, a former French Under 21 international from Lens. Even at the age of thirty-three he was like a breath of fresh air up front.

The most spectacular of the 24 goals that Roger Boli got in 1997/98 was this fine overhead shot against Southend in August 1997 on his way to a hat-trick.

The Sorenson season included a remarkable 7-0 win at Macclesfield in the FA Cup in December 1997 against a team previously unbeaten at home that season. In this picture, Roger Boli is celebrating his goal as Andy Watson tries to join him in celebration.

It didn't quite happen at Old Trafford a month later however, despite a brave battle in front of a crowd of 54,669.

Two more of the players from the continent that brought a new dimension to Walsall under Jan Sorenson – cultured midfielder Jeff Peron and striker Didier Tholot, who chipped in with 5 goals in the last few weeks of 1997/98.

**NEIL JOHNSTON reflects on the brief Walsall managerial reign which ended yesterday**

Sorensen's Saddlers saga . . . Left to right: Day of appointment with chairman Jeff Bonser; an early training session with Derek Mountfield, thumbs-up to the travelling fans after the memorable FA Cup day-out at Old Trafford and receiving an award for performance of the round in the Auto Windscreens Shield

# Nice guy Sorensen –gamble that failed

Once again Walsall will use the close season scouring the market for a new manager.

This time, however, it is entirely their own doing.

The Bescot board's decision to sack Jan Sorensen less than halfway through a two-year contract has left the club in exactly the same position as they were a year ago.

Sorensen was popular with the fans, even if he wasn't with all the players, and he spoke passionately about the challenge of getting the club into the First Division.

So what was it that led Walsall to issuing a terse 17-word statement announcing the former Danish international's departure after just 314 days in the hot seat?

And, more important –where do the club go from here?

There is no doubt that Sorensen's plea for more financial backing, after the 2-1 defeat at Bristol City 11 days ago, was the beginning of the end for the 42-year-old.

But things had been simmering below the surface long before then.

His critics accused him of being tactically naïve while players started to question his training methods as the club flirted dangerously with relegation.

Even when Walsall secured a £500,000 FA Cup date with Manchester United there were rumblings of discontent from within Bescot's corridors of power after Sorensen

told tabloid journalists he was one of the poorest paid bosses in the Football League.

But it was his comments after the match at Ashton Gate that sparked a war of words with club owner Jeff Bonser.

The millionaire businessman, who gambled by handing Sorensen his first managerial job in the English game, might be trying to sell up but he is still very much involved in the day-to-day running of the club.

And his patience with Sorensen was clearly wearing thin last week.

Bonser slammed the manager for the disappointing Second Division fade-out.

He was scathing about the lack of consistency and discipline within the first-team squad and claimed that the club had ploughed an extra £400,000 into the wage bill.

It was no secret that Sorensen wanted more say in the recruiting of players and presented general manager Paul Taylor with a list of 24 names he believed would do a good job.

"Perhaps the problem is more about getting the best out of the players we have, not bringing new ones in," countered Bonser.

The former chairman described Sorensen's appointment back in June as a gamble and it was clearly not paying off.

Even fan power failed to save man who smoked his way through cigarette after cigarette while his players huffed and puffed to

save their Second Division skins.

Despite a dreadful end to the campaign – five points out of a possible 24 – they gave him a rousing reception after last Saturday's defeat by Wycombe while at the same time leaving directors in no mind whom they blamed for the season of struggle.

If he needed a reference there would be no shortage of offers from season ticket holders who stand on Bescot's only terracing.

Perhaps that was his problem. Just maybe he was too nice.

In my 10 years of covering football, Sorensen was without question the most pleasant and approachable manager I have dealt with.

In contrast, Chris Nicholl might not have had as much time for the media but he knew how to get the best out of his players.

Sorensen can at least leave with his head held high. He operated on a low budget – the club did not make a single cash signing while he was in charge – yet he made the club £750,000 from successful runs in the FA Cup and Coca-Cola Cup.

It would have been in excess of £1m if Saddlers had not gaffed in front of their own fans in the Auto Windscreens Shield.

Sorensen certainly deserves credit for keeping faith in teenager Dean Keates who grew stronger and stronger as the season wore on until a knee injury ended it.

But his landslide win in the young player of the year award shows what a midfield talent he is for the future while Jeff Peron,

another one of Sorensen's men, has shown himself to be one of the most skilful players outside the First Division.

Whether Peron is around for the new manager remains to be seen.

In fact the futures of several players are up in the air with Roger Boli and John Hodge also listed.

Former England under-21 players Stuart Ryder and Mark Blake are both out of contract while Andy Watson is also free to leave if he wishes.

As for Didier Tholot and Jean-Jacque Eydelie, both have gone back to Switzerland and may not return.

Although Walsall must share the blame for appointing a manager who had been out of the game for years, they have at least realised their mistake.

The more quickly the new man is in the better for all concerned. It took five weeks to find a successor for Nicholl but I suspect the Bescot board know whom they are after.

With the likes of Manchester City, Stoke and Reading all desperate to return to the First Division next season, he will have his work cut out.

That is why Walsall's fifth manager in eight years should be given financial backing to go out and strengthen the playing squad.

Because for all Sorensen's mistakes, and he made a few, he was let down by certain players who simply did not perform for him when it mattered.

Despite all the cup success, there was no hiding the fact that Walsall finished as low as nineteenth in Division Three in 1997/98. Sorenson had to go, as this report by Neil Johnson confirms.

The new manager for the 1998/99 season was Ray Graydon, a former Aston Villa winger who had a fine reputation as a coach with clubs such as Oxford, Watford, Southampton, QPR and Port Vale.

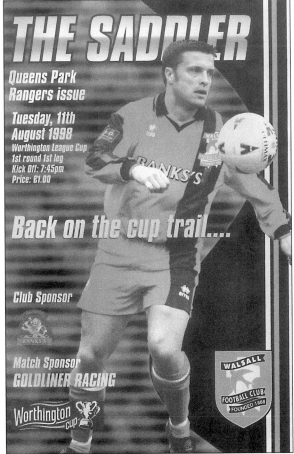

Walsall also kicked off 1998/99 with a new match programme. It had a larger page size than the familiar Permandos publication that had served them for nearly twenty years. Although flashy in appearance, it did not have the same quality content according to many fans.

Happily the team did have sufficient quality and Ray Graydon, with relatively few changes from the previous season's line-up, fashioned a promotion outfit. One spectacular newcomer was swashbuckling striker Andy Rammell, who in his first season banged home 20 goals and was a tremendous crowd pleaser.

# Walsall wonders take first class route to top

## Graydon heroes go up in style as Oldham crumble

### Walsall 3 Oldham 1

WALSALL returned to the Nationwide First Division after an absence of 11 years with a memorable win in front of euphoric supporters at Bescot.

At the same time defeat increased Oldham's fears of relegation, and they must now win their two remaining home games to stay up.

Hundreds of jubilant fans poured on to the pitch at the final whistle to sing and chant until their heroes appeared with glasses of champagne at the back of the main stand.

It was an amazing achievement for the Saddlers' manager Ray Graydon who had spent only £35,000 on one player in building his remarkably successful team.

The Saddlers went in front after 22 minutes when winger Darren Wrack, who had been off the field for 10 minutes having six stitches inserted in a head wound, lashed home an angled shot for his 14th goal of the season.

It was virtually all over in the 34th minute when Walsall increased their lead after a lovely flowing move, their longest serving player, 29-year-old Chris Marsh, bursting into the box to score only his second goal of the season.

Oldham never stopped fighting and were rewarded in the 56th minute when a deflected cross from John Sheridan was met by skipper Lee Duxbury with a header.

A nervous spell followed for the home side, but Icelandic substitute Siggi Eyjolfsson settled the issue in the 76th minute, 10 minutes after going on the pitch.

A pass from Jason Bissett created the opening for Eyjolfsson. The striker, who has played most of his football in American universities, hit a low shot which just beat Kelly.

**Walsall:** Walker, Marsh, Pointon, Henry, Viveash, Roper, Wrack, Steiner, Rammell, Keates, Brissett. Subs: Larusson, Eyjolfsson, Green.
**Oldham:** Kelly, McNiven, Holt, Garnett, Thom, Duxbury, Allott, Sheridan, Beavers, Rickers, Reid. Subs: Tipton, Salt, Sugdeon.
**Referee:** R Styles (Waterlooville).

**SUPERSUB:** Icelander Sigurdur Eyjolfssson celebrates Walsalls third and manager Ray Graydon toasts promotion (inset)

One of the greatest days in Walsall's history was 1 May 1999 when a 3-1 win over Oldham clinched promotion to Division One.

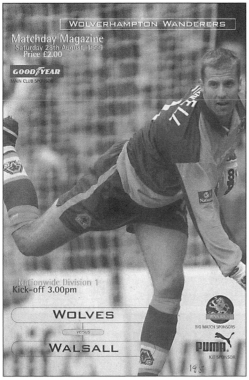

Life turned out to be tough in Division One and Walsall just failed to stay there after a battling 1999/2000 season in which they certainly had their moments, including a remarkable early season win against neighbours Wolves in front of a 24,439 Molineux gate.

# ngry fans protest after Wolves' derby disast

VES players left the field to jeers
rhat a load of rubbish" after Wal-
1ad beaten them at Molineux to
·d their first League win since
1otion.

er Tuesday's Worthington Cup
liation against Wycombe, 
1es needed the tonic of three
ts but found their newly–promot-
·ar neighbours too good for
1 in a competitive derby clash.

1ese are difficult times at
1eux following the £6million sale
1bbie Keane to Coventry and the

| WOLVES | 1 | WALSALL | 2 |
|---|---|---|---|

home crowd were quick to direct their displeasure at the team and managing director John Richards.

The Saddlers needed only three minutes to go in front. Central defender Tony Barras climbed superbly to net with a bouncing header from Darren Wrack's left-wing corner – his second goal in five days.

Wolves had few ideas about getting back into the game but equalised

out of the blue in the 31st minute. Midfielder Carl Robinson rounded keeper James Walker to tap in after Havard Flo had challenged a centre by Darren Bazeley.

Kevin Muscat then hammered a volley off target from a good chance and Wrack lobbed wide at the other end after keeper Mike Stowell had raced off his line to try to meet a through ball by Chris Marsh.

But, after striker Mark Robins had joined team mate Gabor Bukram in the book, the Saddlers regained their lead in first-half injury time. Stowell saved well from a glancing header by Robins from Bukram's centre but Andy Rammell controlled to touch home the loose ball.

Wolves had most of the play in the second half but were never clinical enough to open their opponents up and seriously test Walker.

Their efforts were almost exclu-sively rushed headers from crosses,

with Robinson, Flo and Ne all missing the target with attempts.

Around 300 Wolves fans demonstration outside the after the game.

Wolverhampton: Stowell, Musca Robinson, Curle, Emblen, Osborr Corica, Larkin. Subs: Simpson, N ley, Williams, Mautone.

Walsall: Walker, Marsh, Pointon, Barras, Keates, Bukran, Wrack, mell, Brissett. Subs: Emberson, F Ricketts, Daley, Roper.

Referee: P Robinson (Hull).

Amazingly enough, Walsall have never been beaten in a League game by Wolves, having won twice and drawn four times. In fact, Walsall enjoyed a tremendous record in derby games against all of their West Midlands rivals in 1999/2000. They won both games against West Brom, won one and drew one against Wolves and won one and lost one of their games against Birmingham City. They also gave an outstanding display in drawing with promotion winners Manchester City at Maine Road – had they achieved similar results with teams in the lower half of the table they could well have stayed up. As it was, Walsall went into the last game at Ipswich with an outside chance of avoiding the drop. New midfielders Gabby Bukran (from Hungary) and Pedro Matias (from Spain) made outstanding contributions as did Tony Barras, a former York City defender. All three players stayed at Bescot at the end of the campaign, although there was something of an exodus of players during the summer of 2000.

Despite falling out of Division One, Walsall immediately set about getting together a side capable of taking them straight back up again. General manager Paul Taylor, a former Sheffield Wednesday defender and Gillingham manager, has enjoyed the most successful spell of his career since joining Walsall in 1990. Home and abroad he has found the sort of talent that Ray Graydon could mould into match winners. Here he is pictured with Paul Hall, who arrived from Coventry, initially on loan, in the latter part of 1999/2000.

Jimmy Walker was signed from Notts County in 1993 and in good times and bad has proved himself worthy to follow the tradition of brave and skilful Walsall custodians. By November 2000 he had taken his tally of games past the 300 mark.

There has also been a new upsurge of home-grown talent in recent seasons, amongst them up and coming defenders Ian Roper (left) and Matt Gadsby (right).

Over the past decade the Bescot Stadium has made its mark both with its capacious car parking facilities and splendid conference rooms.

Maybe from the inside it looks rather ordinary when deserted.

Although with a layer of snow it can look quite picturesque.

This is the man who makes things tick off the field. Roy Whalley was a fan who had held down a responsible job at a local school until taking over as secretary in 1986. Although he has had worries to furrow his brow, over the years he has made a major contribution to the club's healthy off-the-field activities, such as the Sunday Market and Sportsman's Evenings.

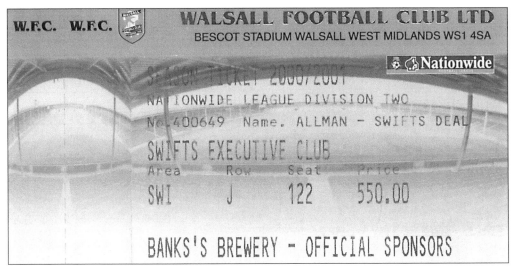

**W.F.C. W.F.C.**

# WALSALL FOOTBALL CLUB LTD
### BESCOT STADIUM WALSALL WEST MIDLANDS WS1 4SA

⚽ Nationwide

SEASON TICKET 2000/2001
NATIONWIDE LEAGUE DIVISION TWO

No. 400649   Name. ALLMAN - SWIFTS DEAL

SWIFTS EXECUTIVE CLUB

| Area | Row | Seat | Price |
|------|-----|------|-------|
| SWI | J | 122 | 550.00 |

BANKS'S BREWERY - OFFICIAL SPONSORS

Fans are in general a happy lot, although a season ticket in 2000 costs rather more than one did in the 1960s.

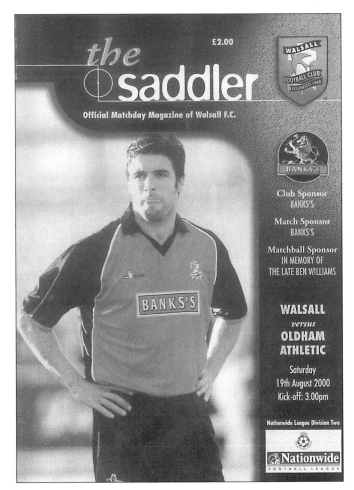

The programme has taken an upturn in the new 2000/01 season with another change of publisher, and the content has improved, though arguably not as much as the team.

This is the team that began 2000/01 full of hope. At the time of writing those hopes have been thus far fulfilled. From left to right, back row: Ian Brightwell, Matt Gadsby, Andy Rammell (now Wycombe), James Walker, Carl Emberson, Gary Birch, Gabor Buckran. Middle row: Bill Jones (youth officer), Mick Kearns (community development officer), Brett Angell, Andy Tilson, Tony Barras, Dion Scott, Ian Roper, Siggi Eyjolfson, Pedro Matias, John Kerr (Centre of Excellence director), Mick Halsall (youth team manager), Duncan Russell (physiotherapist). Front row: Chris Marsh, Dean Keates, Darren Wrack, Jorge Leitao. Ray Graydon (manager), Paul Taylor, (director of football), Tom Bennett, Paul Hall, Darren Byfield, Alfie Carter.

Action from the Bescot Stadium during the match against Wigan in September 2000.